W9-DBU-758

Leaders of the Civil Rights Movement

Other books in the
Profiles in History series:

Black Abolitionists
Black Women Activists
Terrorist Leaders

Leaders of the Civil Rights Movement

Profiles · in · History

Jill Karson, *Book Editor*

Bruce Glassman, *Vice President*
Bonnie Szumski, *Publisher*
Helen Cothran, *Managing Editor*

GREENHAVEN PRESS
An imprint of Thomson Gale, a part of The Thomson Corporation

THOMSON

GALE

Detroit • New York • San Francisco • San Diego • New Haven, Conn.
Waterville, Maine • London • Munich

For more information, contact
Greenhaven Press
27500 Drake Rd.
Farmington Hills, MI 48331-3535
Or you can visit our Internet site at http://www.gale.com

Cover credit: © Picture History
Library of Congress, 14, 19, 46, 57, 97, 127, 172, 201
National Archives, 36, 185

LIBRARY OF CONGRESS CATALOGING-IN-PUBLICATION DATA

Leaders of the civil rights movement / Jill Karson, book editor.
    p. cm. — (Profiles in history)
  Includes bibliographical references and index.
  ISBN 0-7377-2306-8 (lib. : alk. paper)
    1. African American civil rights workers—History. 2. African American civil rights workers—History—Sources. 3. African American civil rights workers—Biography. 4. Civil rights movements—United States—History. 5. Civil rights movements—United States—History—Sources. 6. African Americans—Civil rights—History. 7. African Americans—Civil rights—History—Sources. I. Karson, Jill. II. Series.
  E185.L43 2005
  323'.092'396073—dc22   2003060077

Contents

Chapter 1: Civil Rights Pioneers

1. Frederick Douglass: The Radical as Reformer
The most prominent abolitionist in America rose from slavery to become a powerful black rights spokesman, paving the way for the resistance that would characterize the civil rights era.

2. Sojourner Truth: Abolitionist and Feminist
In nineteenth-century America, Truth defied the notion that ex-slaves and women were powerless. Instead, she transformed herself into a riveting symbol for strong black women.

3. A Plea for Women's Rights
The ex-slave and itinerant preacher implores society to include women's rights in the crusade for black equality.

4. Booker T. Washington and the Tuskegee Institute
Washington's commitment to providing educational opportunities for blacks culminated in the

founding of the Tuskegee Institute, a prestigious
school that generated great controversy.

Chapter 2: Martin Luther King Jr.: Champion of Nonviolent Protest

Foreword

Historians and other scholars have often argued about which forces are most influential in driving the engines of history. A favorite theory in past ages was that powerful supernatural forces—the gods and/or fate—were deciding factors in earthly events. Modern theories, by contrast, have tended to emphasize more natural and less mysterious factors. In the nineteenth century, for example, the great Scottish historian Thomas Carlyle stated, "No great man lives in vain. The history of the world is but the biography of great men." This was the kernel of what came to be known as the "great man" theory of history, the idea that from time to time an unusually gifted, influential man or woman emerges and pushes the course of civilization in a new direction. According to Carlyle:

> Universal History, the history of what man has accomplished in this world, is at bottom the History of the Great Men who have worked here. They were the leaders of men, these great ones; the modelers . . . of whatsoever the general mass of men contrived to do or to attain; all things that we see standing accomplished in the world are properly the outer material result. . . . The soul of the whole world's history, it may justly be considered, were the history of these [persons].

In this view, individuals such as Moses, Buddha, Augustus, Christ, Constantine, Elizabeth I, Thomas Jefferson, Frederick Douglass, Franklin Roosevelt, and Nelson

Mandela accomplished deeds or promoted ideas that sooner or later reshaped human societies in large portions of the globe.

The great man thesis, which was widely popular in the late 1800s and early 1900s, has since been eclipsed by other theories of history. Some scholars accept the "situational" theory. It holds that human leaders and innovators only react to social situations and movements that develop substantially on their own, through random interactions. In this view, Moses achieved fame less because of his unique personal qualities and more because he wisely dealt with the already existing situation of the Hebrews wandering in the desert in search of a new home.

More widely held, however, is a view that in a sense combines the great man and situational theories. Here, major historical periods and political, social, and cultural movements occur when a group of gifted, influential, and like-minded individuals respond to a situation or need over the course of time. In this scenario, Moses is seen as one of a group of prophets who over the course of centuries established important traditions of monotheism; and over time a handful of ambitious, talented pharaohs led ancient Egypt from its emergence as the world's first nation to its great age of conquest and empire. Likewise, the Greek playwrights Sophocles and Euripides, the Elizabethan playwright Shakespeare, and the American playwright Eugene O'Neill all advanced the art of drama, leading it to its present form.

The books in the Profiles in History series chronicle and examine in detail the leading figures in some of history's most important historical periods and movements. Some, like those covering Egypt's leading pharaohs and the most influential U.S. presidents, deal with national leaders guiding a great people through good times and bad. Other volumes in the series examine the leaders of important, constructive social movements, such as those that sought to abolish slavery in the nineteenth century and fought for human rights in the twentieth century. And some, such as the one on Hitler and his henchmen, profile far less constructive, though no less historically important, groups of leaders.

Each book in the series begins with a detailed essay providing crucial background information on the historical period or movement being covered. The main body of the volume consists of a series of shorter essays, each covering an important individual in that period or movement. Where appropriate, two or more essays are devoted to a particularly influential person. Some of the essays provide biographical information; while others, including primary sources by or about the person, focus in on his or her specific deeds, ideas, speeches, or followers. More primary source documents, providing further detail, appear in an appendix, followed by a chronology of events and a thorough, up-to-date bibliography that guides interested readers to further research. Overall, the volumes of the Profiles in History series offer a balanced view of the march of civilization by demonstrating how certain individuals make history and at the same time are products of the deeds and movements of their predecessors.

Introduction

On February 1, 1960, four freshmen from the Negro Agricultural and Technical College in Greensboro, North Carolina, entered Woolworth's Department Store, and, after purchasing several items, took seats at the whites-only lunch counter. When the waitress refused to serve them, the polite but fiercely resolute foursome remained seated until the store closed.

They returned the next day with twenty black students. News of the "sit-ins" galvanized student support across campus, and by the third day, sixty students had joined the movement. Soon, student groups throughout the South were participating in this pioneering form of social protest. Each group was committed to a single goal and a simple code of conduct: They would dress neatly and behave courteously, but they would remain seated at the lunch counter until they were served. They would look straight ahead, and most importantly, they would not respond to taunts, insults, or abuse—no matter how severe—with violence.

Although at times it proved overwhelmingly difficult to remain calm and peaceful, the students persevered. Civil rights activist John Lewis later described the sometimes violent retaliation to which the students were subjected despite their good behavior:

> A group of young white men came in and began pulling people off the lunch-counter stools, putting lighted cigarettes out in our hair or faces or down our

> backs, pouring catsup and hot sauce all over us, push-
> ing us to the floor and beating us. . . . They didn't ar-
> rest a single person that beat us, but they arrested all
> of us and charged us with disorderly conduct.

Within weeks, sit-ins, boycotts, and demonstrations forced the integration of restaurants and other public facilities across the South. The victory was stunning, not only because blacks and whites could sit side by side in restaurants and movie theaters but also because it proved that nonviolent protest and mass action could effect social change.

The college students who dared to challenge segregated lunch counters and others like them were part of what is today called the civil rights movement, the quest by African Americans to gain political, social, and economic equality that peaked between the years 1957 and 1965. Although the sit-in campaigns were indeed pivotal in this turbulent era, the struggle for racial equality had been under way long before four young men refused to give up their seats at Woolworth's.

The Legacy of Slavery

The mass migration of blacks to America began in the early 1600s, when English colonists brought slaves in shackles and chains to North America. Subjugated in every way, slaves were subjected to extreme hardships and denied even the most basic freedoms. At the end of the Civil War, more than 4 million slaves were freed from bondage. Although their hard-won freedom imbued them with a great sense of optimism, blacks were not to see racism and inequality vanquished in that time, especially in the South. Between the years 1865 and 1875—the Reconstruction era—many state and national leaders attempted to ease the slaves' transition to freedom and safeguard their rights through the national legislature. For example, the Thirteenth Amendment meant that blacks were no longer official "property"; the Fifteenth Amendment granted black men the right to vote; and the Civil Rights Acts of 1866 and 1875 affirmed, respectively, that blacks are U.S. citizens and that black males have the right to vote.

These constitutional guarantees were, for the most part, in theory only, as blacks did not come close to enjoying full citizenship and racial equality. Racism was particularly vehement in the South, where slavery had predominated for so many years. White Southerners remained determined to thwart black advances and conspired a variety of means to keep blacks completely disfranchised. One of the most harrowing examples was the birth of the Ku Klux Klan (KKK), an organization that openly rallied its members to attain its chief objective: to retain white supremacy at any cost. Perhaps the ultimate blow to civil rights came in 1896, when the

Segregation through Jim Crow laws was rampant throughout the 1960s, particularly in southern states.

Supreme Court—overturning any gains made during Reconstruction—upheld a law that separated railroad passengers by race in the case of *Plessy v. Ferguson*. This ruling, and its "separate-but-equal" principle, gave white society a legal basis for segregation—and a powerful weapon to deny blacks the same rights enjoyed by their white counterparts.

By 1900, Jim Crow laws—enacted by Southern states to keep hotels, restaurants, theaters, restrooms, and even drinking fountains rigidly segregated—were a deeply entrenched reality. Not only as a result of racist legislation but also as a matter of custom and tradition, Jim Crow kept blacks mired in poverty and bereft of any means to progress socially or economically.

A Changing Outlook

The turn of the century brought a cadre of new leaders ready to launch a full assault against the injustices being inflicted on blacks. In this climate, a handful of activists sought an effective means to harness their political power. In 1909, W.E.B. Du Bois and others founded the National Association for the Advancement of Colored People (NAACP), an organization dedicated to ending segregation and securing civil rights through lobbying, agitation, and legal action. Although reform came slowly, the NAACP relentlessly—and many times successfully—attacked segregation in education, transportation, housing, and public facilities. The group's victories, in turn, spurred more blacks to become politically active, and the campaign for civil rights broadened in the black community.

At the same time, the Industrial Revolution resulted in sophisticated farm equipment that eclipsed black field labor, prompting blacks to travel north in search of jobs. World War I heightened this migration as blacks, eager to work, fled north to take advantage of the burgeoning defense industry. The infusion of blacks, however, aggravated problems, such as a rising postwar unemployment in predominantly white Northern cities.

Although a small but growing number of whites joined the movement to improve conditions for blacks, racial problems prevailed into the 1940s. Then, with America's entry into World War II, came a painful contradiction: Black soldiers fought and died to oppose the racist Nazi regime in Europe and promote freedom abroad. Yet those very ideals for which they had risked their lives were nothing but pretenses at home. Coupled with the redistribution of the black population and surging black aspirations, these developments brought a new sense of urgency to race relations during the mid–twentieth century.

The Birth of a Movement

Two incidents captivated the nation—and catapulted civil rights issues into national prominence. The first spark came when the NAACP won an unprecedented courtroom victory during the early 1950s. For years, the famed lawyer for the NAACP, Thurgood Marshall, had been working to overturn the 1896 *Plessy v. Ferguson* decision that supported segregation. In 1954, Marshall, building on earlier cases, argued *Brown v. Board of Education of Topeka, Kansas*, before the U.S. Supreme Court. On May 17, 1954, the Court ruled that segregation in public schools was illegal. The "separate-but-equal" doctrine established by *Plessy v. Ferguson* was, the High Court decided, not protected by the Constitution.

In presenting the Court's decision, Chief Justice Earl Warren described the damaging effect of racial segregation within the schools:

> Segregation of white and colored children in public schools has a detrimental effect upon the colored children. The impact is greater when it has the sanction

of the law; for the policy of separating the races is usually interpreted as denoting the inferiority of the Negro group. A sense of inferiority affects the motivation of a child to learn. Segregation, with the sanction of law, therefore, has a tendency to inhibit the educational and mental development of Negro children and deprive them of some of the benefits they would receive in a racially integrated school system.

Although *Brown v. Board of Education* officially paved the way for school integration, segregationist policies and traditions did not disappear. Many schools, for example, were slow to comply with the Court's ruling. At the same time, the threat of harassment and even violence kept many blacks from enrolling in predominantly white schools. Meanwhile, the black schools in the South remained run-down, overcrowded, and severely underfunded.

The second major development unfolded in Montgomery, Alabama, where a seamstress named Rosa Parks unwittingly launched a campaign that would create the momentum for the entire civil rights movement. On December 1, 1955, the quiet and unassuming Parks—tired after a day's work—boarded a city bus and made her way to the back rows, where blacks were expected to sit. By custom, too, blacks were to give their seats to white passengers when the front seats were filled. On this evening, however, Parks refused to yield her seat to a white man. Impassive, Parks was arrested.

Leaders of the NAACP saw Parks's arrest as an opportunity to challenge Montgomery's racist bus laws. Almost immediately, black leaders throughout Montgomery rallied behind Parks and the NAACP to demand that the city integrate its buses. They nominated Martin Luther King Jr., a relatively obscure Baptist minister at the time, to organize and lead a citywide bus boycott. Accepting his new position, King stressed his nonviolent approach to civil disobedience, setting a tone that would largely characterize the entire civil rights movement: "There will be no threats and intimidation. . . . Our actions must be guided by the deepest principles of our Christian faith. Love must be our regulating ideal."

Four days after Parks's arrest, the Montgomery bus boycott began—and lasted one long, painful year. Throughout the battle in Montgomery, boycotters endured taunts and harassment—and frequent arrests—yet refused to capitulate. Finally, the federal courts intervened and declared segregation on buses unconstitutional.

The Montgomery bus boycott outcome was important on several counts. First, it marked one more victory over insidious Jim Crow laws. More importantly, it inspired a flood of wide-scale resistance to civil rights abuses throughout the South. The boycott also identified King as a national civil rights leader. Passionate, articulate, and dedicated to nonviolence, he would inspire large-scale participation in the civil rights movement.

By 1957, the crusade for civil rights was well under way. That year, Congress passed the first Civil Rights Act since Reconstruction, which ostensibly strengthened voting rights and also established a civil rights division in the Justice Department. King, too, became highly visible as head of the newly formed Southern Christian Leadership Conference (SCLC), a Christian-based civil rights organization that sought to remove the barriers in society that hindered race relations. Its programs included voter registration drives and direct-action protest. At the same time, the NAACP continued its legal campaigns unabated.

With sit-ins grabbing the media spotlight in 1960, legions of young blacks came forward to work for their cause. They participated in rallies, demonstrations, and boycotts. As expectations swelled, other civil rights organizations rose to prominence. In addition to a number of ad hoc civil rights groups that joined the fray, the Student Nonviolent Coordinating Committee (SNCC) was formed in 1960. Like the SCLC, the group was committed to Christian principles, although it was less patient in its approach to civil rights. Membership burgeoned, too, in the Congress of Racial Equality (CORE), an integrated civil rights organization founded during the 1940s to challenge segregation through peaceful protest. In 1961, CORE garnered massive media attention as it targeted segregation in interstate travel.

Freedom Rides

Although the Supreme Court had banned segregation on buses and in bus terminals and rest areas, change

Freedom Riders sit outside of their destroyed bus in Alabama in 1961 after a white mob brutally attacked the group and burned the bus.

came slowly. Federally mandated integration was largely ignored, and many blacks were too intimidated to exercise their constitutional rights. In response, CORE organized an interracial band of volunteers to participate in what would become known as Freedom Rides. On May 4, 1961, two commercial buses loaded with Freedom Riders embarked on a road trip through the South to force the integration of buses, terminals, and facilities along the way.

Freedom Riders were met with open hostility: They were taunted, threatened, and attacked on several occasions. In one dangerous incident, a busload of Freedom Riders was besieged by an angry white mob that hurled a firebomb into the bus. As the volunteers fled from the burning vehicle, they were attacked and viciously beaten. Across the nation, people were moved by the Freedom Riders' unwavering adherence to their nonviolent philosophy despite brutal attacks against them.

As the 1960s unfolded, civil rights protests continued to spread across the South. SNCC volunteers bravely sponsored their own Freedom Rides, prompting newly elected president John F. Kennedy to dispatch federal marshals to guarantee their safety. Meanwhile, in Albany, Georgia, local black leaders formed the Albany Movement to push for desegregation and voting rights. The Albany Movement generated great enthusiasm and attracted thousands of protesters from various organizations; however, its lack of a unified front rendered it ineffective.

Although the Albany Movement was somewhat of a debacle, King and other black leaders set their sights on a new stage: Birmingham, Alabama, home of the notoriously racist police chief, Eugene "Bull" Connor. King launched his carefully planned campaign in early 1963. When he was later arrested and jailed, he composed his celebrated "Letter from Birmingham Jail," which garnered for him the support of many whites.

Meanwhile, as the protesters continued their deseg-regation campaign in Birmingham, an event occurred that captured the nation's attention: Bull Connor—in full view of television cameras—turned water cannons and snarling police dogs on the nonviolent marchers. Mass arrests followed. The news footage not only spurred more blacks into action, but it also fueled out-rage and sympathy in the white community. After a month of the highly publicized violence, city officials acquiesced to black demands, and the city's public facil-ities were desegregated.

Backlash

As the desegregation movement spread, so, too, did fierce resistance in the white community, especially in the Deep South, where a majority of whites subscribed to the myth of white superiority. With blacks chipping away at discrimination in housing, employment, and quality of education, whites devised ever-bolder strate-gies to sabotage their efforts. These included the for-mation of white citizen councils, legal battles to outlaw the NAACP, and the general threat of violence.

In one highly publicized incident, Governor Ross Barnett of Mississippi attempted to prevent the admis-sion of James Meredith to the University of Mississippi. Similarly, Alabama's newly elected governor, George Wallace—who had unabashedly promised in his 1963 inaugural address to preserve "segregation forever"—tried to block two black students from enrolling at the University of Alabama. In both cases, federal interven-tion guaranteed the students' admission. Later the same year, NAACP leader Medgar Evers was ambushed and shot by a white supremacist. News of Evers's death fur-ther agitated the swelling ranks of civil rights activists.

In light of such events, it became clear that government intervention was necessary to secure civil rights. To that end, black leaders from a broad array of civil rights organizations began plotting a massive campaign to put pressure on the Kennedy administration to pass a major federal civil rights bill. On August 28, 1963, the historic March on Washington brought approximately 250,000 people to the nation's capital. Although a multitude of memorable speakers addressed the crowds, the highlight of the event occurred when Martin Luther King Jr. ascended the platform and delivered his impassioned "I Have a Dream" speech.

The March on Washington generated high hopes as it pushed Congress toward the passage of the Civil Rights Act, broad legislation that outlawed discrimination in employment and in public places, including those that received federal funds. Although many blacks grew disheartened as the proposal seemed to languish in Congress, Lyndon B. Johnson, who became president upon Kennedy's assassination in November 1963, finally pushed the legislation through in 1964.

As changes were taking place, SNCC focused its attention on voting rights. To dramatize its cause, the group launched a series of voter registration drives throughout the South in 1964, placing particular emphasis on Mississippi, where less than 5 percent of the state's eligible blacks were registered to vote. By 1965 the campaign had shifted to Selma, Alabama. Under King's leadership, thousands of demonstrators embarked on a fifty-mile walk from Selma to Montgomery. As the peaceful marchers approached the Edmund Pettus Bridge on March 7, they were blocked by Selma's sheriff, James Clark, who was not only backed up by hundreds of state troopers but was also supported by Governor George Wallace. As a horrified nation watched via television, Clark and his officers—wielding nightsticks and even electric cattle prods—viciously beat the civil rights workers. Even women and children were attacked.

In response to "Bloody Sunday," thousands of people converged on Selma to join the protesters and support their cause—the protection of voting rights for all Americans. In late March, three thousand people reconvened and completed the march to Montgomery, this time under the protection of the Alabama National Guard. Shortly after, on August 6, 1965, President Johnson signed into law the Voting Rights Act.

Black Militancy

As the 1960s progressed, the civil rights movement began to change. Dismantling Jim Crow laws and expanding voting rights had dominated the late 1950s and early 1960s. By 1965, however, poverty and discrimination in the North—insidious albeit not legislated—had come to the forefront of the civil rights debate.

Although King's nonviolent direct action program had been a popular approach to race problems thus far, many blacks were growing frustrated with the slow progress of civil rights. Even organizations like the NAACP came under attack as blacks moved away from tactics they viewed as hopelessly conservative and outmoded. At the same time, many were skeptical that blacks and whites could live together in a racially integrated society. As a generation of blacks redefined themselves, their changing views heralded the rise of more radical strategies—and more militant leaders.

Malcolm X

As King continued to preach passivity and racial harmony, a new black leader rose to the fore. Intense and articulate, Malcolm X urged complete separation from the white race. In direct opposition to King, Malcolm rejected the notion that nonviolence could counter racial problems. Instead, Malcolm rallied disfranchised young blacks to secure their rights "by any means necessary."

After a pilgrimage to Mecca in 1964, he converted to orthodox Islam. Although he continued to advocate militant black nationalism, he no longer promoted complete separation from whites, believing that cooperation between the races was possible.

Malcolm was assassinated in 1965 while addressing a crowd in New York City. His militant philosophy and separatist ideology, however, were perpetuated by a number of organizations. SNCC, for example, hardened its agenda and began advocating a program of "black power," a term that referred not only to taking pride in black culture but also—among the more militant blacks—the complete separation of the races. CORE, too, renounced some of its long-held beliefs in favor of black power. One extremely provocative black nationalist group to emerge was the Black Panthers, originating in Oakland, California, in 1966. Boldly embracing Malcolm X's mantra "by any means necessary," the Black Panthers brazenly carried weapons as they patrolled their neighborhoods.

In this highly charged atmosphere, riots exploded in Watts, a ghetto section of Los Angeles, California, in 1965. The scope of destruction was staggering: Thirty-four people were killed and—following days of looting and burning—property damages were estimated to exceed $40 million. Watts, though, marked only the first of many outbreaks of black violence. Between 1965 and 1968, similar scenes played out in cities across America, where blacks trapped in urban slums lashed out against the poverty and racism in their communities. The worst uprising occurred in Detroit, Michigan, where forty-three people died during the summer of 1967.

Seen on television, the riots ignited a storm of controversy, deepening the chasm between those who believed that civil rights could only be obtained through violence and those who continued to subscribe to a more peaceful philosophy. At the same time, the lure of black nationalist groups—and radical campaigns— proved irresistible to a broad group of blacks who were no longer willing to wait for slow change.

Responding, in part, to the amplified militancy growing within the movement, King and other black leaders launched a campaign to draw national attention to the most pressing problem plaguing the black community: the lack of economic opportunity. As he began organizing a massive "Poor People's March" to highlight working people's economic plight, King traveled to Memphis, Tennessee, to participate in a garbage workers' strike. On April 4, 1968, King was gunned down as he stood on the balcony of his hotel room.

King's death was a crippling blow to the civil rights movement. In an immediate sense, it triggered an explosion of pain, frustration, and violence. Angry and retaliatory, black mobs in many American cities burned and ransacked homes and businesses. More significantly, however, the assassination of Martin Luther King Jr., coupled with the rise of more militant groups and their opposing agendas, led to the dissolution of what had been a unified quest for civil rights.

As the civil rights movement lost momentum during the late 1960s, even the more radical organizations began to wane. Although many groups and organizations that had peaked during the civil rights era continued to operate, the moral outrage and sense of a common cause that had fueled the movement dissipated.

The civil rights movement resulted in many positive gains for blacks, most notably the abolishment of Jim Crow barriers. Due to expanded voting rights, for example, many blacks have been elected to local, state, and national offices. Much progress, too, has been made in the economic sector, largely as a result of increased access to education and economic opportunity. At the same time, however, a disproportionately high number of black Americans remained trapped in urban poverty and a cycle of economic woes. Police brutality against African Americans is another issue that commands frequent attention.

As the twenty-first century unfolds, the struggle to address these and other racial problems will continue to define America. Although Martin Luther King Jr. did not live to see all of his goals met, his prophetic statement that "injustice anywhere is a threat to justice everywhere" reverberates today as minority groups continue to strive for full equality.

1

Profiles · in · History

Civil Rights
Pioneers

Frederick Douglass: The Radical as Reformer

Leslie Friedman Goldstein

Frederick Douglass remains one of the most enduring figures in American history. Born into slavery in 1817, Frederick Douglass seemed destined to a life of servitude and
bondage. Yet in 1838, the determined slave managed to escape to the free North, where his multifaceted career
would take shape: Douglass edited several newspapers, participated in myriad social reform movements, and even
held several political appointments. Perhaps most importantly, Douglass was an extremely articulate and forceful
public speaker. Through his association with William
Lloyd Garrison and other antislavery proponents, Douglass
became a frequent—and fiery—speaker in northern abolitionist circles.

In the following selection, Leslie Friedman Goldstein
discusses Douglass's political philosophy. Douglass rejected
the approach of abolitionist leader William Lloyd Garrison, who favored the use of moral persuasion rather than
force or political action as the means to end slavery. Instead, although he never wavered from his radical goal of
immediate emancipation for all slaves, Douglass sought

Leslie Friedman Goldstein, "Morality and Prudence in the Statesmanship of
Frederick Douglass: Radical as Reformer," *Polity*, Summer 1984, pp. 606–23.
Copyright © 1984 by the Northeastern Political Science Association. Reproduced
by permission.

abolition through political reform. Goldstein is the Judge Hugh Morris Professor of Political Science at the University of Delaware.

❦   ❦   ❦

Frederick Douglass—more by virtue of his influence as a journalist, orator, author, and Republican party activist than because of any government offices he held—deserves to be considered an outstanding black American statesman of the latter half of the nineteenth century. As one of America's most thoughtful statesmen, he pondered at considerable length the tension between pure morality, on the one hand, and political feasibility, on the other. He saw that the statesman needs not only ethical but practical wisdom, for what is politically practicable may not be purely good in the abstract ethical sense. Frederick Douglass, it seems, felt this tension more intensely than most other American statesmen did; certainly he spoke and wrote about it more frequently than most.

The social evils that Douglass targeted for attack were overwhelming in their enormity. He confronted not only the enslavement of millions of blacks with the acquiescence of the white majority, but also confronted widespread denials to free blacks of the right to vote and to bear arms. As a member of this powerless minority struggling against the wrongdoing of the politically and economically powerful majority, Douglass faced a conflict between morality and prudence that was posed about as sharply as it can be posed for a statesman. His thoughtful analysis of this perennial dilemma should be of interest to all those who may be concerned with improving the status of an oppressed

minority within a political system that pays heed to majority will. . . .

Politics and Morality

Frederick Douglass became a political activist virtually
as soon as he escaped from slavery in 1837. That is, he
became a public agitator against the institution of slavery. But in the beginning he did not understand his own
activity to be "political." He knew that he intended to
reform public opinion in order to persuade Americans
to outlaw slavery, but he viewed this as a moral *rather*
than as a political crusade. He associated "politics" with
the greedy quest for the material fruits of public office,
and insisted that religion, not politics, sustains slavery
in that it forms the community's morals and molds
men's consciences. Douglass called Americans to a
"higher and holier warfare" than that they would find
on the battlefield of political action, and warned against
the corrupting lures of the political arena. Instead,
Douglass put his hopes in the press and pulpit for the
moral education of America.

Apparently as a result of contacts with such abolitionists as John Brown, as well as from listening to, and
engaging in, the debates between the Garrisonian Abolitionists (who opposed political action) and the voting-
oriented Political Abolitionists over whether the Constitution was proslavery or antislavery, Douglass came
gradually to an appreciation of the possibility of bringing about moral and social reform *through* politics. In
the process he changed his view of the nature of politics itself. He came to realize that the political task is
not simply to acquire the power of office but that politics is, properly speaking, a moral endeavor. It is concerned with establishing justice and advancing the
common good. Douglass surpassed even his post-
Garrisonian mentor, Gerrit Smith, in his new under-

standing of the moral dimension of politics. In August of 1851, shortly after abandoning the Garrisonian stand *contra* political participation, he wrote to Smith:

> I cannot agree with you . . . in respect to the bounds you set to government. . . . I have a notion that the state—not less than the church should cover the whole ground of morals—incorporating into itself all great moral truths—if government were *righteous* government, there could be little objection to committing education . . . to its charge.

Douglass went on to argue repeatedly throughout his later career that political leadership, no less than religious leadership, must address the moral life of the citizenry, and that the function of laws was not only to coerce but also to educate the people. He made statements to this effect both in theoretical analyses of the nature of law and political leadership, and in analytic descriptions of the Civil War and Reconstruction and post-Reconstruction conflicts. Moral issues, Douglass came firmly to believe, were the very stuff of politics; it was "good versus evil, right versus wrong, liberty versus slavery."

Even at his most anti-political, however, Douglass had never endorsed the philosophical anarchism of his earliest mentor, William Lloyd Garrison. Garrison and the members of his Non-Resistance Society regarded the use of *all* force, even the force of lawful government, as morally wrong. Douglass never precluded the use of government force against evils such as slavery. What had attracted Douglass to the Garrisonian school, at first, was not its philosophy but its persuasive interpretation of the American constitution. Douglass distinguished sharply between lawful and lawless force, arguing that a government that violated its fundamental charter would be "nothing better than a lawless mob, acting without any higher authority than its own impulses or convictions." The nature of the Constitution, embodying the fundamental principles of the regime, was then the pivot on which turned the answer to the most basic of political questions: whether to be a reformer or a revolutionary.

Reform Versus Revolution

Indeed, Douglass characterizes this question as *the* point of controversy between the two abolitionist camps. When he changed over to the Voting Abolitionist camp in 1851, he designated his new position as "one of reform, not of revolution." Paradoxical as it seems, he accompanied this rejection of (non-violent) revolution with a new acceptance of violence as a tactic. In other words, Douglass turned away from the posture a of non-violent revolutionary toward that of a reformer accepting the need for violence. . . .

Douglass' overall strategy can be simply stated: Do not burden yourself with more than is necessary and use all the legitimate weapons available. If the fundamental law of the land overtly, and in its dominant spirit, opposes a direly needed social reform, and would not admit of amendment to the contrary, then the inescapable obligation of a just man is to advocate revolutionary change. He must then agitate for a new fundamental law that would establish the regime on a more just foundation. If, however, the basic principles of the regime, as enunciated in its fundamental law, do not oppose the needed reform and do allow political means for enacting it, it is clearly preferable to work within the law. Public opinion must be moved to support the reform, and the law is a powerful vehicle for moving public opinion.

Thus, Douglass argued that, "the great gulf between voting and non-voting abolitionists" had developed from disagreement over whether or not the Constitution was pro-slavery. His changed perception of the

Constitution—from the view that it was a pro-slavery document in intent and in legal content to the one that it was anti-slavery in both respects—greatly influenced how he weighed the slavery elements of the American regime against the freedom-favoring elements. . . .

Indeed, so convinced was Douglass of the usefulness of having the Constitution on his side, that he stopped characterizing it as *pro*-slavery months before he became convinced that it was *anti*-slavery. He would rather be silent than hand over the Constitution on a silver platter to his enemies. Douglass' perception of the Constitution eventually changed when he recognized that deliberate omissions of words must be taken into account in interpreting documents, considered the Constitution's own wording, saw that the founders expected slavery soon to end under the Constitution, and realized that slavery had been much weaker during the early years of the Republic than it had been in recent decades. Douglass then began to call for political action, for change *within* the existing political system, to end slavery.

As soon as Douglass could honestly convince himself—and this took him at least two years of careful study—that the basic principles of the American regime could be viewed as supporting, or even requiring, the abolition of slavery, he happily cast off the additional burden of overthrowing the whole American government. He began to argue that the political and legal principles on which this country stood could not tolerate the continuation of slavery.

The political and historical circumstances in which Douglass was operating made revolutionary solutions problematic. While it is generally simpler to change a particular social institution than to destroy and reconstitute an entire government, the Garrisonian revolutionary option—which was the major abolitionist alternative during the pre–Civil War years—made matters worse by urging secession. The Garrisonians not only denounced the Constitution but also asked that the Union be split into at least two fragments so that the morally pure need have "no union with slaveholders."

The longer Douglass pondered the secession solution the less workable he found it to be. By 1855, the prospect of massive slave escapes or revolts, even if the North left the Union and encouraged them, appeared remote. It followed that breaking the Union because of opposition to slavery would leave the slaves to their masters. Southern slavemasters would remain as untroubled by American abolitionists as were the slaveholders of Brazil and Cuba. To counsel *this* kind of overthrow of the government would not only place added burdens upon the abolitionist cause; it would practically result in abandoning the goal of abolition.

Abolition Above All Other Reforms

Douglass' strategy of avoiding unnecessary burdens in attaining the desired reform may seem to be inconsistent with his active involvement in a wide array of other reform movements—temperance, Irish Liberation, opposition to capital punishment, women's rights. From a lifetime perspective, however, his participation in these movements was of secondary importance. Even the women's rights movement, for which he worked throughout his adult life, did not distract him from his primary commitment.

Douglass had a sharply delineated set of priorities. None of the social evils against which he campaigned could approximate the horrors of slavery, and he made this explicit from the start. He noted, for example, in 1846:

> It is common . . . to distinguish every bad thing by the name of slavery. Intemperance is slavery; to be

deprived of the right to vote is slavery, says one; to have to work hard is slavery, says another. . . .

I do not wish for a moment to detract from the horror with which the evil of intemperance is contemplated—not at all; nor do I wish to throw the slightest obstruction in the way of any political freedom that any class of persons in this country may desire to obtain. But I am here to say that I think the term slavery is sometimes abused by identifying it with that which it is not.

Just as he himself put the abolition of slavery—because of the incomparable evils of that institution—above all other social reforms in significance and urgency, so he expected other American abolitionists to do the same. He had no sympathy for the women abolitionists who allowed themselves, in his view, to be carried away by their own desire for equal status to such an extent that they would split the American Anti-Slavery Society over the issue of the treatment of its women members. Similarly, Douglass was disappointed with the leaders of the feminist Equal Rights Association (Lucy Stone, Elizabeth Cady Stanton, and Susan B. Anthony) when they refused to endorse the Fifteenth Amendment on the grounds of its failure to give the vote to women. Douglass was willing to continue to work separately for the cause of black suffrage and for the cause of women's suffrage, but he was not willing to have them merged into a single cause. That would have increased the odds against public acceptance of the suffrage package; "all or nothing" was decidedly not Douglass' strategy as a reformer.

This is not to say that he refrained from advocating drastic and radical reforms; the point is that he was willing to push for them one at a time. The abolition of slavery was a radical change and so was the granting of suffrage to freed men who had been out of slavery for only five years. Douglass labored hard for each of these, but he did not insist that the former was not worth taking if the latter were not simultaneously granted. True to this pattern, he returned to participation in the women's suffrage movement *after* the Fifteenth Amendment had been adopted. . . .

Frederick Douglass

It should be emphasized that Douglass' preference for taking first things first did not imply an acceptance of "gradualism" as a reform strategy. Justice being his measure, and confronted as he was with "monstrous iniquity" in his own homeland, he spoke proudly of his "radical opinions" and his "ultraist" behavior. He did not shy away from the fact that, as an abolitionist, he was calling for a genuinely radical transformation of the American social system.

Not only did Douglass have radical goals, he favored radical measures for attaining those goals. His preference for drastic or shocking tactics was linked to his concern with reshaping public opinion. Drastic tactics—on *either* side—served to awaken public interest. Once people started paying attention, Douglass believed, the evils of slavery would, as it were, speak for themselves.

> I like radical measures, whether adopted by Abolitionists or slaveholders. . . . I am delighted to see any effort to prop up the system on the part of the slaveholders. It serves to bring up the subject before the people, and hasten the day of deliverance.

This, of course, was the basic reasoning behind "agitation" as a reform method; the public mind should be agitated to the point where it would recognize the horrors of slavery. Because America was a democratic republic, once public opinion favored the abolition of slavery, the battle would be won.

Parties and Politicians
Douglass' entry into the fray of party politics did not moderate his interest in the radical or the extreme measure. He viewed his activities in party politics as simply another segment of his overall effort to move public sentiment toward the abolitionist position. His efforts in party politics were really a series of attempts to radicalize the party conflict. He wished the electoral conflict to center around the most fundamental issues facing the regime. In a letter written before the war, he observed: "We have turned Whigs and Democrats into Republicans, and we can turn Republicans into Abolitionists."

As a radical agitator, Douglass welcomed the extremism, the aggressive audacity, of the proslavery forces. Measures such as the Congressional "gag rule," the infamous declaration of Judge [Roger B.] Taney that Negroes had no rights in America, the display of brute force within the very halls of Congress, the bloody battle over Kansas—all these, according to Douglass, "served as fuel to the fire" which was heating the nation toward the conflagration that would put an end to slavery. Douglass gave the brazen Kansas-Nebraska Act, and its cavalier repeal of the Missouri Compromise, the credit for having brought Abraham Lincoln onto the national political scene, and for having convinced Northern public opinion that the slavery question was no longer "to be slighted or ignored.". . .

Despite this preference for radical improvements in the existing polity, Douglass understood it to be an axiom of electoral politics that a party must have "not only ideas, but numbers." He recognized that the degree of compromise, or of moderation of principles, suitable to party action was of necessity different from the level of compromise appropriate for a personal morality. He explained the distinction as follows:

> There is a place in the world for individual action, and a place for political party action. In the field of moral action, a man may place his standard as high as he pleases. In this field, one man with the right and the true is a majority. He may invoke his standard of religious perfection . . . but in politics a man to be of any practical use to his country or the world, must work with the multitudes.

Any political party, if it meant to have an impact, could not appeal only to a moral elite; it would have to be able to attract a majority or a near-majority of the voters. (A near majority might pose enough of a threat that the other party would be influenced to change its stance on crucial issues.) This interpretation of the role of morals in party politics in a democracy came to Douglass gradually. A chronological retracing of his involvement in the American party system illustrates the dilemma he confronted as a radical reformer attempting to influence electoral politics.

Douglass perceived the potential of the ballot as a weapon for social change long before he actually entered the political battlefield. This first phase of his involvement with politics might be seen as a period of intensely interested ambivalence. His views on the Constitution pulled him in one direction; his interest in politics, in another. From 1848, when the controversy over the Wilmot Proviso gave birth to the Free Soil Party, until Douglass openly abandoned Garrisonianism in 1851, he belied his own principled rejection of participation in party conflict by his editorial support for, and his active personal involvement in, both the Liberty Party and the Free Soil Party Conventions.

During this phase Douglass personally opposed voting because he still believed that the Constitution was proslavery (and that therefore any elected official would be sworn to uphold slavery), but he praised the Free Soil Party for publicizing the anti-slavery cause and for giving an anti-slavery option to those who (mistakenly) believed in voting. He endorsed the Free Soil candidates in the manner of a physician who concedes that cigars will harm the patient less than cigarettes. Douglas himself maintained Garrisonian purity and refused to vote, but he advised his politically active readers that a Free Soil vote would be a lesser evil than contributing to the extension of slavery.

Both his praise and his criticism of the Free Soil campaign of 1848 indicate that Douglass saw that party's value as agitational rather than electoral. He credited it with rallying new members to the anti-slavery cause, and with teaching a lesson to certain recalcitrant politicians. He was disappointed, however, with its watering down of the abolitionist doctrine. For, by its willingness to compromise for the sake of winning allies, the party had muddied the former clarity of the Abolitionist position and confused the public.

> Upon the whole it has left the public mind in a more difficult state to deal with than it found it. It found it agitated, divided, and the lines drawn distinctly but has left it dull, stupid, undefined, and indifferent. Instead of making the task of the abolitionist lighter, it has increased his burdens. . . .

However, some of his statements show that [the] matter of providing anti-slavery voters a vehicle to express their viewpoint was not so important to Douglass as his expectation that this anti-slavery party would eventually lead to an even more radically anti-slavery party. The problem was that the more people the Free Soil Party tried to represent, the more diluted and nebulous its anti-slavery principles became. As its electoral chances improved, its educational or agitational role declined. Douglass watched sadly as, in 1849, the Free Soil Party admitted Democrats into its ranks. His comment at this time presents an interesting contrast to his more mature views on the need for compromise in politics quoted above.

> Why should Free Soilers wish to unite with any party, on any basis, were it not from some such motive [of expediency]? Two or three are sufficient to make a party, if a party must be made; one is sufficient to stand alone if he is only satisfied of the truth of his principles.

The Outside Agitator

During the years 1848–1851, Douglass stayed aloof from politics by refusing to vote, and in this way paid his obeisance to moral principle. He also paid his tribute to numbers by endorsing the Free Soil candidates for the 1848 election. For the 1852, 1856, and 1860 elections, Douglass developed a new position to cope with the numbers vs. principle dilemma. He stayed outside the Free Soil and then the Republican party until late in the campaigns, claimed to be a member of the Liberty or Radical Abolitionist Party (a very small group mostly in New York), and denounced the Free Soilers (and later the Republicans) for not being sufficiently anti-slavery. In this way, he upheld the anti-slavery principles, and tried to move the more mainstream party toward his preferred position. However, each time, shortly before the election, Douglass shifted his ground and endorsed the more mainstream party candidates (Free Soil in 1852 and Republican in 1856 and 1860). These shifts in August of 1852 and 1856 and in October of 1860 indicate that Douglass would not altogether reject practical wisdom in favor of moral fervor. He knew that numbers do count in elections and that the results of elections could do great harm or considerable good to the slave's cause.

Douglass persisted in this in-again-out-again pattern, instead of remaining within the Free Soil or Republican Party, perhaps because he believed that he could influence the party more as an outside agitator than as a member of its organization. It is conceivable that his formal membership in the party would have been viewed as a tacit endorsement of Free Soil, rather than Radical Abolitionist, principles.

The dramatic transformation of Abraham Lincoln, from a presidential candidate only moderately antislavery to the president who emancipated the slaves, seems to have profoundly altered Douglass' attitude toward political parties. Convinced now of the importance of winning elections, and indelibly impressed with the fact that the Republican Party had freed four million of his oppressed brethren, Douglass became a Republican Party stalwart and "stumped" for the party in every post-bellum campaign until his death. Although he was no longer an outsider, Douglass did not give up the gadfly aspect of his former role. He now worked from *within* the party ranks to radicalize the Republican platform as described above. . . .

In order to rid America of slavery Lincoln needed "the earnest sympathy and the powerful cooperation of his loyal fellow countrymen. Without this *primary* and *essential condition to success*, his efforts must have been in vain and utterly fruitless." (Emphasis added.) Douglass the agitator was free to stir up fierce passions, to anger his opponents. But Douglass the agitator knew that Lincoln the statesman did not have the same freedom. Douglass acknowledged that, "had [Lincoln] put the abolition of slavery before the salvation of the Union, he would have inevitably driven from him a powerful class of the American people and rendered resistance to rebellion impossible." Profound social change in a republic requires not only agitators and radicals of Douglass' ilk, but also statesmen of Lincoln's stature. The latter recognize, as Douglass pointed out, that as statesmen they *must* consult the country's sentiment. If they move too far ahead of it, they simply cannot attain success. Measured against genuine abolitionists, Lincoln had seemed "tardy, cold, dull, and indifferent." But measured against popular sentiment, "he was swift, zealous, radical and determined."

Lincoln's example taught Douglass the lesson of democratic statesmanship: the indispensability of popular support for the successful initiation of great social change. He continued to introduce moral principles into discussions of public affairs, but he did so and performed his role as agitator in the postwar years from within the Republican Party.

Sojourner Truth: Abolitionist and Feminist

Silvana Siddali

In the following selection Silvana Siddali explains that Isabella Bomefree was born a slave in New York around 1797. One of the defining elements of her life was watching her siblings sold to other slave owners, and then later, experiencing the sale of several of her own children. According to Siddali, Isabella became free in 1828, and in 1843, she changed her name to Sojourner Truth after an inner voice told her to do so.

After changing her name, Truth became an itinerant minister, and her travels brought her into contact with some of the most important civil rights leaders of the time. As a consequence, she began to speak about women's and racial equality in her preaching and became known as both an abolitionist and a suffragist. Siddali reports that Truth published her autobiography, the *Narrative of Sojourner Truth*, in 1850, and during the Civil War, she met Abraham Lincoln. After the war, she worked to assist former slaves, and she inspired thousands of freedmen to establish homesteads in Kansas. Truth continued to travel and speak until

Silvana Siddali, "Sojourner Truth," *American Eras*, 8 vols. Farmington Hills, MI: Gale Research, 1997–1998. Copyright © 1997–1998 by The Gale Group. Reproduced by permission.

her death in Battle Creek, Michigan, in November 1883. Silvana Siddali writes historical essays for the Gale Group.

🦇 🦇 🦇

Isabella Bomefree was born around 1797 on the estate of a Dutch patroon in Ulster County, New York, where her parents were slaves. Her first language was Dutch, and she would speak with an accent all her life. One of the formative events of her early childhood was witnessing her parents' grief over the loss of children who had been sold away. When she was nine Isabella herself was sold, and she was sold several more times in her early life. She worked from 1810 to 1827 in the household of John J. Dumont of New Paltz, New York. There she married a fellow slave named Thomas, with whom she had at least five children: two daughters and a son were sold away from her. When Dumont demanded that she serve another year after New York declared slavery illegal, Bomefree escaped. That year she also became a Christian; her religious commitments, combined with a deep knowledge of the Bible, would influence her profoundly throughout her life. Isaac and Maria Van Wagener took her in, and she adopted their last name. With the help of Quaker friends she successfully sued her former owner for the return of her son Peter, who had been sold illegally to an Alabama planter.

Freedom and Faith

Around 1829 Isabella Van Wagener moved to New York City with her two youngest children, Peter and Sophia. She joined the Methodist Church and adopted the evangelistic, "perfectionist" religious beliefs that inspired her own mystical faith. Throughout her life she would hear voices and see visions. In New York she met Elijah Pierson, a wealthy and erratic social reformer whose primary work was with prostitutes, and joined Pierson and his wife in preaching in the streets. In the 1830s Van Wagener moved to a commune in Ossining, New York, remaining there for five years. She eventually returned to New York City, where she lived quietly and attended the African Zion Church, until 1843, when an inner voice told her to change her name to Sojourner Truth. She became an itinerant minister, traveling around the Connecticut River valley to preach, sing, pray, and evangelize at camp meetings, in churches, or wherever she could find shelter and an audience. Her message was that God was loving and perfect, and that human beings had nothing to fear from him. She said often that "God is from everlasting to everlasting" and that "Truth burns up error." She believed that God was present everywhere and that all beings lived in him as "fishes in the sea." In the winter of 1843 Sojourner Truth moved to the Northampton Industrial Association, another utopian community, where she lived until 1846. There she met important members of the abolitionist movement, including Frederick Douglass and George Benson, brother-in-law of the antislavery leader William Lloyd Garrison. As a result of this experience, abolitionism and women's rights became important to Sojourner Truth and were always expressed in her preaching. She never compromised on the importance of these causes, disagreeing with abolitionists such as Douglass, who maintained that equality for women ought to be subordinated to the elimination of slavery.

Autobiography and Speeches
In 1850 Truth published her autobiography, ghostwritten by Olive Gilbert. She supported herself by selling *The Narrative of Sojourner Truth* at women's rights meet-

ings for twenty-five cents a copy. Truth's "Ar'n't I a Woman?" speech at the Akron Women's Rights Convention in 1850 has gone down in history as one of the most significant expressions of the combined abolitionist and women's rights movement. When Truth rose to speak she was severely heckled; undaunted, she pointed out that as a female slave she had experienced the profound grief of having her own children sold away and had had to work like a man all her life; she then asked, "And ar'n't I a woman?" She left the stage to tumultuous applause. At a women's rights convention in Indiana she responded to charges that she was a man posing as a woman by baring her breast to her accusers.

Sojourner Truth

Civil War and Freedpeoples' Rights

In the mid 1850s Truth moved with her daughters to Battle-Creek, Michigan, a center of religious and anti-slavery reform movements. There she joined a commune called Harmonia. During the Civil War she met President Abraham Lincoln and worked on freed slaves' relief projects such as the Freedmen's Hospital and the Freedmen's Village at Arlington Heights, Virginia. One of her grandsons served in the celebrated black regiment, the Fifty-fourth Massachusetts Volunteers. In an article that appeared in *The Atlantic Monthly* during the war the antislavery writer Harriet Beecher Stowe immortalized Truth as the "Libyan Sybil"; the name would be associated with Truth for the rest of her life. After the war Truth worked tirelessly to assist former slaves; in 1870 she sent a petition to Congress, signed by hundreds of supporters, pleading for the allocation of government lands in the West to former slaves. Although Congress took no action on the petition, her outspoken support of western migration inspired thousands of former slaves to establish homesteads in Kansas. She traveled throughout Kansas and Missouri, exhorting the former slaves to "Be clean! for cleanliness is godliness." She also continued to speak to white audiences in the Northeast, preaching her message of a loving God and advocating temperance, woman suffrage, and equal rights for blacks.

Final Years

In the mid 1870s Truth's autobiography was revised and republished. She continued to travel and speak on social reform issues such as temperance as long as she was able, and she received hundreds of visitors in Battle Creek until her death on 26 November 1883. Her funeral was said to have been the largest ever held in Battle Creek.

A Plea for Women's Rights

Sojourner Truth

Throughout her life, Sojourner Truth spoke out on a variety of causes, including abolition and later the rights of freed slaves. At the same time, she was a fierce defender of women's rights, a movement that grew in part out of the antislavery movement. Truth delivered the speech that follows, which addresses society's unequal treatment of black women, at the First Annual Meeting of the American Equal Rights Association on May 9, 1867. Although she was uneducated, Truth's oratory was artful. Speaking forcefully, she roused the audience with her plaintive plea for women's rights, lamenting that "there is a great stir about colored men getting their rights, but not a word about the colored women."

❦ ❦ ❦

My friends, I am rejoiced that you are glad, but I don't know how you will feel when I get through. I come from another field—the country of the slave. They have got their liberty so much good luck to have

Sojourner Truth, speech before the First Annual Meeting of the American Equal Rights Association, New York, May 9, 1867.

slavery partly destroyed; not entirely. I want it root and branch destroyed. Then we will all be free indeed. I feel that if I have to answer for the deeds done in my body just as much as a man, I have a right to have just as much as a man. There is a great stir about colored men getting their rights, but not a word about the colored women; and if colored men get their rights, and not colored women theirs, you see the colored men will be masters over the women, and it will be just as bad as it was before. So I am for keeping the thing going while things are stirring; because if we wait till it is still, it will take a great while to get it going again. White women are a great deal smarter, and know more than colored women, while colored women do not know scarcely anything. They go out washing, which is about as high as a colored woman gets, and their men go about idle, strutting up and down; and take it all, and then scold because there is no food. I want you consider on that, chil'n. I call you chil'n; you are somebody's chil'n, and I am old enough to be mother of all that is here. I want women to have their rights. In the courts women have no right, no voice; nobody speaks for them. I wish woman to have her voice there among the pettifoggers. If it is not a fit place for women, it is unfit for men to be there.

A Plea for Equal Rights

I am above eighty years old; it is about time for me to be going. I have been forty years a slave and forty years free and would be here forty years more to have equal rights for all. I suppose I am kept here because something remains for me to do; I suppose I am yet to help to break the chain. I have done a great deal of work; as much as a man, but did not get so much pay. I used to work in the field and bind grain, keeping up with the cradler; but men doing no more, got twice as much pay;

so with the German women. They work in the field and do as much work, but do not get the pay. We do as much, we eat as much, we want as much. I suppose I am about the only colored woman that goes about to speak for the rights of colored women. I want to keep the thing stirring, now that the ice is cracked. What we want is a little money. You men know that you get as much again as women when you write, or for what you do. When we get our rights we shall not have to come to you for money, for then we shall have money enough in our own pockets; and may be you will ask us for money. But help us now until we get it. It is a good consolation to know that when we have got this battle once fought we shall not be coming to you any more. You have been having our rights so long, that you think, like a slave-holder, that you own us. I know that is hard for one who has held the reins for so long to give up; it cuts like a knife. It will feel all the better when it closes up again. I have been in Washington about three years, seeing about these colored people. Now colored men have the right to vote. There ought to be equal rights now more than ever, since colored people have got their freedom. I am going to talk several times while I am here; so now I will do a little singing. I have not heard any singing since I came here.

Booker T. Washington and the Tuskegee Institute

Emma Lou Thornbrough

Booker T. Washington was born into slavery in 1856. After the Civil War ended and he had attained his freedom, he founded the Tuskegee Institute, a vocational school that promoted Washington's lifelong belief. Through self-improvement and the acquisition of practical skills such as sewing and farming, blacks could progress economically and therefore elevate their standing in society. While many in the white community embraced Washington's utilitarian philosophy, a host of black critics deemed it an inadequate—if not harmful—approach to advancing black causes. At the core of this rift stood the scholar W.E.B. Du Bois, who proclaimed that Washington's focus on industrial education and conciliation with white society thwarted black intellectual and political growth—and ultimately perpetuated blacks' second-class citizenship.

The following biographical sketch, excerpted from Emma Lou Thornbrough's *Booker T. Washington*, chronicles Washington's illustrious life and, notwithstanding the controversy he generated, his formidable achievements as a race leader.

Emma Lou Thornbrough, "Introduction," *Booker T. Washington*, edited by Emma Lou Thornbrough. Englewood Cliffs, NJ: Prentice-Hall, Inc., 1969. Copyright © 1969 by Prentice-Hall, Inc. All rights reserved. Reproduced by permission.

🐾 🐾 🐾

The child who was later to be known as Booker T. Washington was born on April 5, 1856. His birth and the conditions of his early years were typical of the slave system. His mother, Jane, was a slave and the cook on a small plantation in the back country of Virginia. His father was a white man, but except that he came from a neighboring plantation, the child knew nothing of his identity. In fact he was never even sure of the year of his own birth. His mother called him Booker, but he had no last name until he went to school. When he realized that all of the other children at school had a "second" name and the teacher asked him his, he invented the name Washington, and henceforth he and his brothers (John, who was also the son of a white man, and James, who was adopted) used the name.

In his autobiography, *Up From Slavery*, which gives an unforgettable picture of his childhood, Washington said that as a boy he tried to imagine what it would have been like to be a white boy with an honored family name and distinguished ancestry. He remarked that white people who constantly called attention to the "moral weaknesses" of Negro youths and compared them unfavorably with white youths did "not consider the influence of the memories which cling about the old family homesteads." A proud family history and the desire to perpetuate it gave white boys a stimulus to succeed which Negroes lacked. On the other hand, Washington said, if he had been "a member of a more popular race," he might have been inclined to rely upon his ancestry and color to do for him what he should have done for himself.

Certainly, even as a boy, he did not allow the circumstances of his birth to deter him from moving "up from slavery." In fact, the entire story of his life became an impressive example of the American success story—a story of remarkable achievements in the face of almost insurmountable obstacles.

After the Civil War ended, Jane and her children moved to Malden, West Virginia, where Washington Ferguson, a former slave to whom she was now married, had found employment in the salt mines. At the age of nine Booker also went to work in the mines. But in spite of gruelling labor he managed to enroll for a time in a local school for Negroes. In 1871 he left the mines to go to work as a houseboy in the home of General Lewis Ruffin, owner of the mines. His association with Mrs. Ruffin, a strict New Englander, was to be one of the important influences in his life. From her he learned respect for cleanliness and pride in a job well done.

At sixteen the boy took what was probably the most decisive step in his life when he resolved to enter Hampton Institute in Virginia. Hampton, which had opened in 1868, was the product of the inspiration and effort of General Samuel C. Armstrong, the son of American missionaries in Hawaii. Armstrong was convinced that the ultimate solution of the problems of the Negro freedmen lay in education—but education of a practical and utilitarian nature which would teach the skills necessary for earning a livelihood and at the same time develop character and morality.

Young Washington, who traveled most of the distance from Malden by foot, arrived at Hampton penniless and dirty. Nevertheless, he was able to persuade the authorities to admit him and to give him a janitorial job which helped to pay his expenses. As a student he received instruction in basic academic subjects and also learned practical lessons in agriculture. He also learned some even more basic lessons in personal cleanliness and conduct, and by participating in the debating society, he began to develop his talent for public speaking. But the most important part of his experience at Hampton was the association with General Armstrong, whom Washington described in his autobiography as "a great man—the noblest, rarest human being that it has ever been my privilege to meet." Not only did Armstrong become Washington's model as an educator; in later years he also helped his pupil gain access to the northern philanthropist who played an indispensable role in the development of Tuskegee.

For three years after graduation from Hampton, Washington taught school in Malden and then spent a year at Wayland Seminary in Washington, D.C. His experience here reinforced attitudes which had been inculcated at Hampton. He was somewhat disdainful of the purely academic training offered at Wayland and more firmly convinced of the value of a system which emphasized practical skills, self-help, and the dignity of labor. From Wayland he returned to Hampton for two years as a teacher.

Tuskegee

Then in 1881, on the recommendation of General Armstrong, he went to Tuskegee in Macon County, Alabama, to become principal of a new school. The Alabama legislature had authorized the establishment of a normal school to train colored teachers and had appropriated $2,000 for salaries. When Washington arrived, however, there were no buildings, nor even land upon which to build. The school was at first conducted in a shanty loaned by the local Negro church. But, in spite of seemingly insurmountable obstacles, Washington acquired land, built buildings, secured equipment, and recruited teachers and students. The next fifteen years of his life were spent in creating in the Black Belt of Alabama an institution which was in large part a replica of

Hampton. There was one significant difference: Hampton had been founded by white persons and the principal and part of the staff were white, while Tuskegee was an all-Negro institution.

The bricks for the buildings at Tuskegee were made by the students, and much of the construction was done by student labor. A large part of the food consumed by the students was grown and prepared by them. In the classrooms academic subjects were infused with materials and examples of a utilitarian nature and related to the actual experience of the students. All boys received "industrial training" in such fields as brickmaking, carpentry, blacksmithing, dairying, and agriculture. Girls studied cooking and sewing. Much emphasis was placed on teaching personal hygiene and manners and on character building. Tuskegee was nondenominational, but all students were required to attend chapel daily and a series of religious services on Sunday. Most impressive were the Sunday evening meetings at which Washington addressed the students.

By 1906 enrollment at Tuskegee had grown to 1,500, and the staff numbered 155. By the time of Washington's death the school had an endowment of about $2 million, property worth more than $1.5 million, and an annual budget of $300,000. In addition to regular classes Tuskegee extended its influence through short courses for farmers, the annual Farmers' Conference, the Rural School Extension Department, and the Tuskegee Negro Conferences. Tuskegee graduates taught in all of the states in the South and in Africa.

Meanwhile, soon after going to Tuskegee, Washington had married his boyhood sweetheart, Fannie N. Smith of Malden. She died two years later, leaving an infant daughter, Portia. In 1885 Washington married Olivia Davidson, who had been assistant principal at Tuskegee and who had contributed almost as much as

Washington himself to establishing the school and raising funds during its early years. Two sons, Booker Tal-
iaferro, Jr., and E. Davidson, were born of this marriage. The second Mrs. Washington died in 1889. In
1893 Washington was married a third time—to Mar-
garet Murray, a graduate of Fisk University, who had
come to Tuskegee in 1889 as lady principal. She was
her husband's enthusiastic supporter in all his endeav-
ors and played an important role at Tuskegee.

The Atlanta Speech

From the earliest years at Tuskegee, Washington had
gone on northern tours, seeking funds and sometimes
making speeches on behalf of his school and explaining
his educational doctrines. In 1884 his reputation as a
speaker brought him an invitation to address the annual
meeting of the National Educational Association at
Madison, Wisconsin. But his first important opportunity to speak in the South came when he was designated
to give an address on behalf of Negroes at the opening
of the Cotton States and International Exposition in
Atlanta on September 18, 1895. The speech, given before a racially mixed audience, was directed principally
to the white listeners. Although it lasted only about fifteen minutes, it contained the basic ideas on race relations which have ever since been associated with the
name of Washington. Both the speech and the speaker
were received with tumultuous applause by the audience. White newspapers North and South, gave the address extended coverage and praised Washington edito-
rially. Almost   overnight   the   principal   of   Tuskegee
found himself a national figure, hailed as spokesman
and leader of Negro Americans.

After the address honors came thick and fast. The following year Harvard University conferred an honorary
M.A. degree upon Washington, the first such degree it

had awarded to a Negro. In 1898 President McKinley visited Tuskegee while on a tour of the South. In 1899 white friends sent Washington on a European tour for a much needed vacation. Everywhere he went he was lionized. He even had tea with Queen Victoria.

After the Atlanta Address, Washington was in such demand as a public speaker that he spent a substantial part of each year on the lecture circuit. His activities were so fully reported in the press that he became one of the best-known Americans of his day. As his fame increased, there were demands for his autobiography. In 1901 *Up From Slavery* appeared in book form after having first been serialized in *The Outlook*. This account of his trials and successes immediately became a best seller in the United States and was ultimately translated into more than a dozen foreign languages. Emmett Scott, Washington's secretary, later wrote that *Up From Slavery* brought more money to Tuskegee than any other effort of Washington's. It was the reading of this book, more than anything else, which caused Andrew Carnegie and Henry H. Rogers of the Standard Oil Company to become interested in Tuskegee.

Washington (center, seated) poses with the Tuskegee Institute faculty. Andrew Carnegie (seated, second from right) donated generously to the school.

Washington's Influence

In spite of the adulation which was heaped upon him, Washington's position with white southerners was always somewhat precarious. This was vividly demonstrated by the furor which ensued when it became known that President Theodore Roosevelt had entertained the Negro educator at a family dinner at the White House. For weeks—and even months—southern newspapers and southern politicians placed up the incident as evidence that Roosevelt and Washington were seeking to break down social barriers between whites and Negroes. But the real significance of the incident was the fact that the President of the United States was consulting with a southern Negro about political matters. Throughout Roosevelt's administration he relied heavily upon Washington's advice in making appointments of whites as well as Negroes in the South and consulted with him on other matters relating to racial policies. Behind the scenes Washington worked for the election of William Howard Taft as Roosevelt's successor in 1908, and he continued to wield important influence during Taft's administration. In spite of his deprecatory attitude toward politics Washington had far greater political power than any other Negro of his time and probably more influence at the White House than any white southerner. But his influence was sharply reduced when Wilson, a Democrat, was elected in 1912.

Washington also showed a remarkable capacity for winning the trust and support of leading industrialists and financiers. Most significant perhaps was his relationship with Andrew Carnegie, who became Tuskegee's most important donor and who bestowed upon Washington a gift of money which guaranteed him and his wife an income for life. Washington was also on friendly terms with William H. Baldwin, Jr., vice-president of the Southern Railway, Henry H. Rogers of Standard

Oil, merchants John W. Wanamaker and Robert C. Ogden, Collis P. Huntington, the railroad magnate, and Julius Rosenwald of Sears, Roebuck and Company. Some of these men, although northerners, had interests in the rising industries of the New South, a fact which Washington undoubtedly kept in mind when expressing his views on labor relations and economic policies in general. Washington also successfully cultivated good relations with conservative southern political leaders like Governor Thomas G. Jones of Alabama, whom he persuaded Theodore Roosevelt to appoint to the federal bench. He also knew well such men as Walter Hines Page and Lyman Abbott, who as editors and publishers were influential in molding public opinion. Many of these men served on the board of Tuskegee and gave money to the school. Washington was also instrumental in persuading some of them to endow other agencies for the promotion of Negro education in the South. Among these were the Rockefeller-endowed General Education Board, which was concerned with higher education, and the Rosenwald Fund, the Anna T. Jeanes Fund, and the Phelps-Stokes Fund, all of which were concerned with the education of rural Negroes. It was unlikely that any Negro institution would become a recipient of white philanthropy unless Washington approved.

So great was Washington's influence in the white world that Negroes in politics, education, and other fields were dependent upon his good will for appointments. But at the same time Washington's influence with whites depended in part upon the support which he had from the Negro community. Although always preserving a modest and self-effacing facade, he worked assiduously to maintain his reputation as race leader. He organized the National Negro Business League and served as its president, and for a number of years he dominated the Afro-American Council, an organization dedicated to working against racial discrimination. He used the Negro press and other publications for promoting his ideology and his personal prestige.

Washington's Critics

But from the time he first won national recognition some Negroes dissented from his doctrines and refused to acknowledge him as the leader of his race. In 1903 the existence of Negro opposition received increasing attention among whites when W.E.B. Du Bois publicly took issue with Washington. Du Bois, who was the first Negro to receive a Ph.D. degree from Harvard, symbolized the Negro intellectuals who were critical of Washington's educational doctrines and his apparent acquiescence in disfranchisement and segregation. Shortly before this, William Monroe Trotter, a Harvard graduate, had begun publication of the Boston *Guardian*, a militant newspaper which has as its *raison d'etre* opposition to Washington and which subjected him to virulent abuse. In 1905 Du Bois, Trotter, and other Negro intellectuals formed the Niagara Movement to fight uncompromisingly for full citizenship for Negroes. More threatening to Washington's position was the founding in 1909 of the National Association for the Advancement of Colored People, a biracial organization in which the white philanthropist Oswald Garrison Villard, who had been a supporter of Tuskegee, played a prominent role. Du Bois became executive secretary of the NAACP and editor of its publication, *The Crisis*.

In the face of rising opposition Washington made strenuous efforts to maintain his position and to discredit his critics. Until his death he continued to enjoy the support of most of the philanthropists and the white press. When he died in 1915, he was eulogized as few Americans have ever been. Nevertheless in his last years, as a result of the rise of the NAACP and the victory of Wilson and the Democrats, the power and prestige which he had wielded diminished, somewhat.

Washington's Core Philosophy

His speeches and published writings reveal Washington as a man of a few basic ideas which he constantly reiterated. His fundamental philosophy appears to have crystallized early and to have changed very little. He was a prolific writer, but all his writings say essentially the same thing.

At the outset of his career, Washington later wrote, he recognized that if Tuskegee was to be a success he must win the support of three groups—the "best class" of southern whites, northern whites with a philanthropic interest in the South, and members of his own race. It is evident that in everything he wrote he weighed the effect of his words on these three groups. He was remarkably successful in winning white support, and his success must be attributed in large part to the fact that the views which he expressed on almost all subjects—political, economic, social, as well as racial— were essentially the views of contemporary white Americans. There is little that is original in his thought, and his style is pedestrian and heavy with clichés. At first reading he appears to have been a simple man with simple ideas, but a more careful reading reveals a subtlety not at first apparent. The ambiguity and ambivalence in nearly everything he said or wrote were no doubt the result of the peculiar position he held in relation to whites and Negroes. His writings show little evidence of intellectual or scholarly profundity, but they reveal a man with an understanding of the psychology of the white society in which he lived and with which he had to deal.

He appeared to accept the traditional southern view of the American past, including the Negro past. He once compared the slave system to a prison, but he usually emphasized the benevolent aspects of slavery. He appears to have had no bitter personal memories of his slave origins, and he told many stories of the loyalty of slaves to their masters and the mutual affection between slaves and members of the master's family. He spoke of the "naturally cheerful disposition of the African," and his delineation of "Negro character" corresponded closely with the stereotype accepted by his white contemporaries. Much of his popularity rested on the "darkey" stories with which he delighted white audiences—stories in which the Negro was depicted as a lovable, sometimes shrewd, but essentially childlike figure. He frequently expressed the opinion, shared by most of his generation, that Reconstruction had been a tragic mistake. In *Up From Slavery* he says that even as a child he felt that Reconstruction policy toward Negroes had rested on a false foundation and was "artificial and forced"—that it was a policy imposed by white northern politicians who "wanted to punish the Southern white men by forcing them [Negroes] into positions over the heads of the Southern whites." It would have been better for the Negro in the long run, he felt, if there had been educational or property requirements for voting. Instead of concentrating on political activity and looking to the federal government for aid and protection, the recently emancipated slaves would have done better to have directed their energies toward securing an education and property.

The core of Washington's philosophy was that the progress of Negroes in all other fields depended upon economic progress. The opportunity to earn a living and acquire property was more important than the right to vote. Throughout his career he tried to impress upon the masses of Negroes that "in agriculture, in industries, in commerce, and in the struggle toward economic success, there were compensations for losses they had suffered in other [i.e., political] directions." Negroes had to learn that "economic efficiency was the foundation for every kind of success." If they made themselves economically indispensable, they would gain political and other rights. "No race that has anything to contribute to the markets of the world is long in any degree ostracized," he said in the Atlanta Address. He frequently asserted that if a Negro held the mortgage on a white man's house it was unlikely that the white man would try to prevent him from voting.

"Cast down your buckets where you are," he advised Negroes in the Atlanta Address, and he continued to the end of his life to insist that Negroes had better economic opportunities in the South and encountered less economic discrimination there than in the North. He also thought that Negroes were better off in the South because there were fewer temptations to immorality and extravagance than in northern cities.

Along with emphasis upon economic progress, he preached the doctrine of thrift and the dignity of labor. He frequently berated Negroes for their tendency to waste their money on "the ornamental gewgaws of life." The opportunity to earn a dollar in a factory was of more importance to the Negro, he said, than the opportunity to spend a dollar in the opera house.

The educational system which he developed at Tuskegee was a natural outgrowth of these views. Slavery had meant work, and in the early years of freedom, said Washington, Negroes had too often looked upon education as means of escaping from work. Tuskegee, like Hampton, stressed the dignity of work and the moral value of working with the hands. Above all, Washington sought to stress the *practical* and to relate the education of the students to the world in which they lived.

W.E.B. Du Bois: Scholar and Activist

Jacob U. Gordon

W.E.B. Du Bois stands out as one of the most influential African American leaders of the nineteenth and twentieth centuries. His contributions are monumental: A prolific writer, scholar, educator, and social activist, Du Bois worked tirelessly to dismantle institutional racism, advocating social protest and agitation to this end. In 1905 he founded the Niagara Movement, a civil rights forerunner to the National Association for the Advancement of Colored People (NAACP). As a founding member of the NAACP, Du Bois helped build the organization into a powerful force in the black protest movement.

The following article by Jacob U. Gordon enumerates Du Bois's scholarly and organizational achievements, focusing on his tremendous impact on the NAACP, which ultimately paved the way for subsequent victories in the civil rights movement. Gordon is professor of African and African American studies at the University of Kansas. He is the author of twelve books, including *The African American Male: His Present Status and Future* (1994) and others that center on racial issues.

🐝 🐝 🐝

Jacob U. Gordon, "Black Males in the Civil Rights Movement," *The Annals of the American Academy of Political and Social Science*, vol. 569, May 2000, pp. 43–45.

One of the most prominent and influential black leaders of the twentieth century, William Edward Burghardt Du Bois, was a free black born on 23 February 1868, in Great Barrington, Massachusetts, the year of President Andrew Johnson's impeachment. Educated at Fisk University, a predominantly black private university (A.B., 1888), the University of Berlin, and Harvard University (A.B., 1890; Ph.D., 1896), Du Bois went on to become an articulate intellectual and distinguished scholar. His first book, *Suppression of the African Slave Trade to the United States, 1638–1870* (1969), was a pioneering book that, until recently, was considered the definitive study of the slave trade in the United States. It was based on his 1896 doctoral dissertation. In addition to his writing, Du Bois held teaching positions at Wilberforce University, the University of Pennsylvania, and Atlanta University.

Du Bois is best remembered as the leader of those early-twentieth-century black intellectuals who challenged the accommodationist leadership of Booker T. Washington. Washington, of course, stressed the concept of industrial and vocational education for blacks, conciliation with the white South, and submission and silence as to black civil and political rights. Writing in *The Souls of Black Folk* (1903), Du Bois asserted that the Washington program practically accepted the alleged inferiority of black people. The function of education, according to Du Bois, was to train individuals for social leadership. Blacks would continue to be led by whites until an African American intelligentsia (what Du Bois called the "talented tenth") was allowed to emerge. By straitjacketing blacks with vocational education, as opposed to traditional liberal arts education, such an emergence would never occur. "Mr. Washington's programme," Du Bois commented, "ignores the Negro's right to vote, his right to attend universities to secure a liberal arts education and his right to share equally in the American dream."

The NAACP

In 1905, Du Bois founded the Niagara Movement and, five years later, became one of the prominent leaders of the National Association for the Advancement of Colored People (NAACP). Throughout this time, he continued to hammer away at Washington's leadership of American blacks. Du Bois advocated and genuinely believed in what modern sociologists called "cultural pluralism." Rejecting the concept of the melting pot, he realized that complete amalgamation of the races in America probably would never occur. He insisted, however, that blacks wanted to be both black and American, maintaining their racial identity and integrity while associating with and participating in American culture to the fullest extent. As early as 1897, Du Bois had written that "one feels [the Negro's] two-ness—an American, a Negro, two souls, two thoughts, two unreconciled strivings, two warring ideals in one dark body. He simply wishes to make it possible for a man to be both a Negro and an American without being cursed and spit upon."

A major influence over all twentieth-century black protest, Du Bois worked within the NAACP until after World War II, serving as editor of the organization's monthly magazine, *The Crisis*, from 1910 to 1934. As the director of publications and research and editor of *The Crisis*, Du Bois made significant contributions to the growth and influence of the NAACP. For example, in 1919, the NAACP published *Thirty Years of Lynching in the United States, 1889–1918*, which estimated that 3224 blacks had been lynched during this period.

He was also devoted to the cause of pan-Africanism and, as a result of his persistent attacks upon colonial rule in Africa, is often referred to as the "Godfather of African Independence." During his later life, Du Bois became increasingly discouraged by the lack of genuine racial progress in the United States. As a result, he emigrated to Ghana at the age of 93. A close friend of Ghanaian leader Kwame Nkrumah, Du Bois became a citizen of Ghana two months before his death in 1963.

Aside from Du Bois, the first group of NAACP officials, including the organization's first president, Moorfield Storey, were whites. Bringing most of the black intellectuals from the Niagara Movement into the new group with him, Du Bois was assured an important role in the NAACP.

Notwithstanding contemporary accusations of conservatism and Uncle Tomism leveled by many young black militants, the NAACP was in the vanguard of the black struggle for civil rights and equality in America. Founded in 1909 in response to the prevailing pattern of American segregation, disfranchisement, and racial violence, the NAACP from the outset has been an interracial organization.

By maintaining a strong lobby in Washington, the NAACP has successfully campaigned for laws designed to protect and, when necessary, extend the rights of African Americans. Equally significant have been the NAACP's legal battles in the courts against unjust laws and inadequate enforcement of constitutionally guaranteed rights. The organization's most notable success came as a result of its steady and skillful assault on public school segregation, an assault that culminated in 1954 when the Supreme Court of the United States, in *Brown v. Board of Education*, declared that racially segregated schools are "inherently unequal." Legal victories such as these set the stage for the subsequent civil rights revolution during the 1960s.

The Immediate Program of the American Negro

W.E.B. Du Bois

As a founding member of the NAACP and the editor of
the organization's magazine, the *Crisis*, W.E.B. Du Bois
frequently elucidated the NAACP's strategy to achieve citizenship rights for all Americans. As he became more
pointed in his views, however, Du Bois went beyond the
NAACP's formal program and supported even broader
means of securing equality in housing, voting, employment, education, and transportation, for example. In 1916,
the *Crisis* included the following statement by Du Bois.
With his characteristic incisiveness, Du Bois advocates a
broad program of action—breaking down obstructions to
civil rights through legislative means and broadening educational opportunities, for instance—to uplift blacks and
promote social and political equality.

❧ ❧ ❧

The immediate program of the American Negro
means nothing unless it is mediate to his great ideal and

W.E.B. Du Bois, "The Immediate Program of the American Negro," *The Crisis*,
vol. IX, April 1915, pp. 310–12.

the ultimate ends of his development. We need not waste time by seeking to deceive our enemies into thinking that we are going to be content with a half loaf, or by being willing to lull our friends into a false sense of our indifference and present satisfaction.

The American Negro demands equality—political equality, industrial equality and social equality; and he is never going to rest satisfied with anything less. He demands this in no spirit of braggadocio and with no obsequious envy of others, but as an absolute measure of self-defense and the only one that will assure to the darker races their ultimate survival on earth.

Only in a demand and a persistent demand for essential equality in the modern realm of human culture can any people show a real pride of race and a decent self-respect. For any group, nation or race to admit for a moment the present monstrous demand of the white race to be the inheritors of the earth, the arbiters of mankind and the sole owners of a heritage of culture which they did not create, nor even improve to any greater extent than the other great division of men—to admit such pretense for a moment is for the race to write itself down immediately as indisputably inferior in judgment, knowledge and common sense.

The equality in political, industrial and social life which modern men must have in order to live, is not to be confounded with sameness. On the contrary, in our case, it is rather insistence upon the right of diversity;— upon the right of a human being to be a man even if he does not wear the same cut of vest, the same curl of hair or the same color of skin. Human equality does not even entail, as is sometimes said, absolute equality of opportunity; for certainly the natural inequalities of inherent genius and varying gift make this a dubious phase [*phrase*]. But there is a more and more clearly recognized minimum of opportunity and maximum of freedom to be, to move and to think, which the modern world denies to no being which it recognizes as a real man.

These involve both negative and positive sides. They call for freedom on the one hand and power on the other. The Negro must have political freedom; taxation without representation is tyranny. American Negroes of to-day are ruled by tyrants who take what they please in taxes and give what they please in law and administration, in justice and in injustice; and the great mass of black people must stand helpless and voiceless before a condition which has time and time again caused other peoples to fight and die.

The Negro must have industrial freedom. Between the peonage of the rural South, the oppression of shrewd capitalists and the jealousy of certain trade unions, the Negro laborer is the most exploited class in the country, giving more hard toil for less money than any other American, and . . . [has] less voice in the conditions of his labor.

In social intercourse every effort is being made to-day from the President of the United States and the so-called Church of Christ down to saloons and bootblacks to segregate, strangle and spiritually starve Negroes so as to give them the least possible chance to know and share civilization.

These shackles must go. But that is but the beginning. The Negro must have power; the power of men, the right to do, to know, to feel and to express that knowledge, action and spiritual gift. He must not simply be free from the political tyranny of white folk, he must have the right to vote and to rule over the citizens, white and black, to the extent of his proven foresight and ability. He must have a voice in the new industrial democracy which is building and the power to see to it that his children are not in the next generation trained to be the mudsills of society. He must have the right to social intercourse with his fellows. There was a time in the atomic individualistic group when "social intercourse" meant merely calls and tea-parties; to-day social intercourse means theatres, lectures, organizations, churches, clubs, excursions, travel, hotels,—it means in short Life; to bar a group from such methods of thinking, living and doing is to bar them from the world and bid them create a new world;—a task to which no single group is today equal; it is to crucify them and taunt them with not being able to live.

What now are the practical steps which must be taken to accomplish these ends?

First of all before taking steps the wise man knows the object and end of his journey. There are those who would advise the black man to pay little or no attention to where he is going so long as he keeps moving. They assume that God or his vice-gerent the White Man will attend to the steering. This is arrant nonsense. The feet of those that aimlessly wander land as often in hell as in heaven. Conscious self-realization and self-direction is the watchword of modern man, and the first article in the program of any group that will survive must be the great aim, equality and power among them.

Dismantling Obstructions

The practical steps to this are clear. First we must fight obstructions; by continual and increasing effort we must first make American courts either build up a body of decisions which will protect the plain legal rights of American citizens or else make them tear down the civil and political rights of all citizens in order to oppress a few. Either result will bring justice in the end. It is lots of fun and most ingenious just now for courts to twist law so as to say I shall not live here or vote there, or marry the woman who wishes to marry me. But when to-morrow these decisions throttle all freedom and overthrow the foundation of democracy and decency, there is going to be some judicial house cleaning.

We must *secondly* seek in legislature and congress remedial legislation; national aid to public school education, the removal of all legal discriminations based simply on race and color, and [of] those marriage laws passed to make the seduction of black girls easy and without legal penalty.

Third the human contact of human beings must be increased; the policy which brings into sympathetic touch and understanding, men and women, rich and poor, capitalist and laborer, Asiatic and European, must bring into closer contact and mutual knowledge the white and black people of this land. It is the most frightful indictment of a country which dares to call itself civilized that it has allowed itself to drift into a state of ignorance where ten million people are coming to believe that all white people are liars and thieves, and the whites in turn to believe that the chief industry of Negroes is raping white women.

Fourth only the publication of the truth repeatedly and incisively and uncompromisingly can secure that change in public opinion which will correct these awful lies. THE CRISIS, our record of the darker races, must have a circulation not of 35,000 chiefly among colored folk but of at least 250,000 among all men who believe in men. It must not be a namby-pamby box of salve, but a voice that thunders fact and is more anxious to be true than pleasing. There should be a campaign of tract distribution—short well written facts and arguments—rained over this land by millions of copies, particularly in the South, where the white people know less about the Negro than in any other part of the civilized world. The press should be utilized—the 400 Negro weeklies, the great dailies and eventually the magazines, when we get magazine editors who will lead public opinion instead of following afar with resonant brays. Lectures, lantern-slides and moving pictures, co-operating with a bureau of information and eventually becoming a Negro encyclopedia, all these are efforts along the line of making human beings realize that Negroes are human.

Constructive Programs

Such is the program of work against obstructions. Let us now turn to constructive effort. This may be summed up under (1) economic co-operation (2) a revival of art and literature (3) political action (4) education and (5) organization.

Under economic co-operation we must strive to spread the idea among colored people that the accumulation of wealth is for social rather than individual ends. We must avoid, in the advancement of the Negro race, the mistakes of ruthless exploitation which have marked modern economic history. To this end we must seek not simply home ownership, small landholding and saving accounts, but also all forms of co-operation, both in production and distribution, profit sharing, building and loan associations, systematic charity for definite, practical ends, systematic migration from mob rule and robbery, to freedom and enfranchisement, the emancipation of women and the abolition of child labor.

In art and literature we should try to loose the tremendous emotional wealth of the Negro and the dramatic strength of his problems through writing, the stage, pageantry and other forms of art. We should resurrect forgotten ancient Negro art and history, and we should set the black man before the world as both a creative artist and a strong subject for artistic treatment.

In political action we should organize the votes of Negroes in such congressional districts as have any number of Negro voters. We should systematically interrogate candidates on matters vital to Negro freedom and uplift. We should train colored voters to reject the bribe of office and to accept only decent legal enactments both for their own uplift and for the uplift of laboring classes of all races and both sexes.

In education we must seek to give colored children free public school training. We must watch with grave suspicion the attempt of those who, under the guise of vocational training, would fasten ignorance and menial service on the Negro for another generation. Our children must not in large numbers, be forced into the servant class; for menial service is still, in the main, little more than an antiquated survival of impossible conditions. It has always been as statistics show, a main cause of bastardy and prostitution and despite its many marvelous exceptions it will never come to the light of decency and honor until the house servant becomes the Servant in the House. It is our duty then, not drastically but persistently, to seek out colored children of ability and genius, to open up to them broader, industrial opportunity and above all, to find that Talented Tenth and encourage it by the best and most exhaustive training in order to supply the Negro race and the world with leaders, thinkers and artists.

For the accomplishment of all these ends we must organize. Organization among us already has gone far but it must go much further and higher. Organization is sacrifice. It is sacrifice of opinions, of time, of work and of money, but it is, after all, the cheapest way of buying the most priceless of gifts—freedom and efficiency. I thank God that most of the money that supports the National Association for the Advancement of Colored People comes from black hands; a still larger proportion must so come, and we must not only support but control this and similar organizations and hold them unwaveringly to our objects, our aims and our ideals.

Ida B. Wells: Antilynching Crusader

Linda O. McMurry

In the post-Reconstruction South, racial strife—and the practice of lynching—abounded. A particularly heinous incident in Tennessee in 1892 resulted in the lynching deaths of three black businessmen, one of whom was a friend of Ida B. Wells. A journalist at the time, Wells reacted to the atrocity by penning a scathing editorial. Although this journalistic attack angered many in the white community, it ultimately launched what would become a nationwide campaign against the lynching of black men. As the fiery spokesperson of the movement, Wells dedicated her life to exposing—and arousing public opinion against—this form of terrorism against blacks. The following selection, excerpted from Linda O. McMurry's *To Keep the Waters Troubled*, recounts Wells's life and antilynching efforts, as well as her participation in other reform movements, including suffrage and other women's rights causes.

Linda O. McMurry, *To Keep the Waters Troubled: The Life of Ida B. Wells*. New York: Oxford University Press, 1998. Copyright © 1998 by Linda O. McMurry. All rights reserved. Reproduced by permission of Oxford University Press, Inc.

After the Civil War, many extraordinary African Americans rapidly rose from obscurity and bondage to incredible positions of fame and autonomy. Outstanding ability often overcomes adversity, but rarely have so many climbed so far so quickly with so little help. Among the numerous stories of personal courage and fortitude, few are more heroic than that of Ida B. Wells. Born into slavery and orphaned as a teenager, Wells took charge of herself and her younger siblings, supporting them by teaching. In an age when women were often considered dependent on male protectors, both the insecurity and the liberation of relative independence profoundly shaped Wells as she sought to balance her desires and multiple duties. She felt a keen sense of responsibility to a number of people and causes. Often she was asked to choose between competing ideals: support of black "manhood" and the need for strong black women; race unity and belief in the oneness of humanity; political realities and personal integrity; racial uplift and class identity; tolerance and high moral standards; integration and black autonomy; nurturing her family and crusading for justice. Wells supported many reform movements only to discover that white leaders of such causes as woman suffrage and temperance expected her to put their movements' interests ahead of the struggle for black rights. This she refused to do. For almost half her life she remained single and struggled with the social expectations of womanhood, while emerging as an activist more militant than most of her male colleagues.

Wells was barely twenty years old when she sued a railroad company in 1883 for expelling her from a first-class coach. Her account of the case launched her into a part-time career in journalism, which became her full-time vocation when the white school board in

Memphis dismissed her for publicly criticizing its actions. As editor of the Memphis *Free Speech*, Wells began a crusade against lynching. Her editorials infuriated local whites, who eventually closed down her newspaper and forced her exile. Moving to New York, she immersed herself in the antilynching cause, which included two British lecture tours.

For several years in the 1890s, no African American, except for Frederick Douglass, received more press attention than Ida B. Wells. She played a role similar to the aging abolitionist, arousing British public opinion against the new evil of lynching as Douglass had against the old evil of slavery. Both were entertained by royalty and other prominent people and launched British movements that brought unwanted attention to America's racial problems. When Douglass died in 1895, Wells was his logical heir apparent; they had closely collaborated on several projects. She was better known than W.E.B. Du Bois and more ideologically compatible with Douglass than Booker T. Washington—the two men who eventually became the main contenders to fill Douglass's shoes. However, Wells had a major problem: She was a woman.

The Emasculation of Black Men
In post-Reconstruction America, black women faced a serious dilemma. White southerners were attempting to repeal the advances made by African Americans by stripping black men of not only their power but also their pride. Southern white men defined manhood partly as the ability to protect their "helpless" women. To deny black manhood, they forbade any sexual contact between black men and white women, while claiming for themselves the right of sexual access to black women. Lynching was a major tool for the emasculation of black men. To support their men and to counteract

the challenges to black manhood, black women usually assumed some of the roles played by white women in this patriarchal society. They, too, were expected to be submissive and to lend support rather than to provide leadership. For a woman to be spokesperson and leader for African Americans belittled black "manhood."

The first step by Wells into the role of spokesperson grew out of her rage over the lynching of a close friend in 1892. The horror of that event focussed Wells's attention and anger on the evil of mob violence. She correctly diagnosed the major purpose of lynching in the 1890s as an antidote to black success rather than the resulting black degradation, a form of racial terrorism. Few African Americans were lynched prior to the Civil War because of slaves' monetary value as well as slavery's effectiveness as a system of racial control and domination. After emancipation, white southerners increasingly used lynching to intimidate black men. The practice reached its peak in the 1890s, the same time whites were forging a new system of racial subordination based on segregation and disfranchisement. That decade also witnessed the growing use of rape charges as the justification for lynching.

Wells's Militancy

Wells's attack on the lynch law focused on refuting the prevailing notion that lynching was needed to defend white women from the lust of black men. She was not the first to attack the rape myth, but she became the loudest and most persistent voice for truth. Thus while white men proclaimed themselves protectors of their women's purity, a woman emerged as the defender of black men's honor and lives. This role reversal caused controversy, and Wells provoked animosity as well as admiration. Further undermining her ability to follow expected gender roles was her assertiveness. Her uncompromising militancy made most male leaders look timid. Although most African Americans supported Wells's efforts, from the beginning of her career some black men challenged her femininity. Their attacks sometimes took the form of vocalizing doubts about her purity and propriety, both of which were crucial to her ability to support herself as well as to advance the cause of her people. Wells, therefore, struggled to balance her need to be perceived as a "lady" with her natural militancy.

Although Wells chafed under the restrictions resulting from her gender, she consistently placed race interests above gender issues. Feeling a divided duty to the fight for equal rights by women and by African Americans, she participated in both movements. Black women of her era typically saw racism as a greater evil than sexism, and Wells was not an exception. More than most women of either race, however, she was ambivalent about her gender identification. Her actions challenged gender roles largely because she identified with men rather than women. Wells often seemed to view other women as if she were an outsider who found most women to be weak, shallow, and petty. As a result she got along better with men, who elected her to offices in national organizations while women's groups did not. Nevertheless, she encountered male resentment of her leadership roles and, consequently, felt alienated somewhat from both sexes. Being a black woman activist required a delicate balancing act, and Wells could not walk the tightrope as deftly as some other women.

Her militancy also placed Wells out of sync with the growing moderation of black leaders. After causing her exile from Memphis, Tennessee, her temper led her tongue to alienate even those who were ideologically compatible. Wells was a person, however, who could not be ignored. Very little happened in the struggles for black and women's rights without her participation from the 1890s to her death in 1931. She was active in the founding of numerous organizations, such as the NAACP, and collaborated with many leaders, including Du Bois, William Monroe Trotter, Henry McNeal Turner, and Marcus Garvey. At the same time, she worked with such white women activists as Susan B. Anthony and Jane Addams. In the end she chastised most coworkers for compromising and founded her own groups in her new hometown of Chicago. Her inability to work successfully with most people meant that she became alienated from movements and failed to get appropriate credit for her work both during her life and for a long time afterward. Nevertheless, she played a very important role in history by being, in her own words, the "disturbing element which kept the waters troubled."

Her personal life was almost as frustrating as her public one. Wells sought to play numerous roles simultaneously and was often torn between her desires and her responsibilities. Forced at sixteen to become the head of the household, she became accustomed to a degree of independence that would have been threatened by marriage. Her relationships with men were problematic personally as well as professionally. For almost half her life she remained single, unable to find a man she could respect who did not threaten her independence. When she finally found a man with whom she was compatible, Wells was in her thirties and at the peak of her career. Marriage and motherhood limited— but did not stop—her activism. Soon after her first child was born, her suffragist friend Susan B. Anthony complained that Wells "had a special call for special work" and that motherhood gave her "a divided duty." She fought until her death to fulfill her duties as woman, African American, and activist.

Profiles · in · History

Martin Luther King Jr.: Champion of Nonviolent Protest

Martin Luther King Jr.

Thomas Siebold

As America grappled with rising racial tension in the early part of the twentieth century, a host of leaders emerged who would shape and lead the modern civil rights movement. Yet few did more to alter the face of race relations during these turbulent years than Martin Luther King Jr. His rousing speeches virtually ignited the movement, and his commitment to nonviolence set the tone that would characterize the entire era.

In the following selection, editor and author Thomas Siebold provides an overview of King's life. Exposed to racism in the South at an early age, King developed a sense of the injustice that prevailed in America. He emerged from his schooling as a minister with a gift for oratory and a strong belief in the tenets of Mohandas Gandhi and Jesus Christ. He never wavered in his pursuit of nonviolent resistance, even when confronted with violent reactions from whites. His efforts were central in the passage of the two most sweeping civil rights bills in the nation's history: the Civil Rights Act of 1964 and the Voting Rights Act of 1996.

Thomas Siebold, "Martin Luther King Jr.: Crusader for Social Justice," *Martin Luther King Jr.*, edited by Thomas Siebold. San Diego, CA: Greenhaven Press, 2000. Copyright © 2000 by Greenhaven Press. Reproduced by permission.

Martin Luther King Jr. was born on January 15, 1929, in Atlanta, Georgia. Martin was the second of three children born to Reverend Martin Luther King Sr. [known to his family as "Daddy King"] and Alberta Williams King. Daughter Willie Christine was one year older than Martin, born in 1928, and Alfred Daniel, called A.D., was one year younger, born in 1930. The King children grew up in a pleasant Victorian house on Atlanta's Auburn Avenue, located in a comfortable neighborhood that contained some of the city's most successful black-owned businesses.

Throughout his life, even as a youngster, Martin disliked violence, preferring his ability to persuade and influence others with language. Although Martin's early years were comfortable, secure, and somewhat sheltered from Jim Crow abuses, he was nonetheless introduced to the ugliness of bigotry at an early age. Certainly Martin, like all black Southern children, knew that there were places blacks could not go: swimming pools, rest rooms, water fountains, certain seats on the bus, and particular restaurants and businesses. But first-hand, personal discrimination hit him directly when the mother of his two white preschool playmates told Martin that he could not play with her sons anymore because he was black. Martin's mother consoled him but the sting of rejection and injustice hit him hard.

Like his father, Martin Luther King Jr. liked school. He attended Young Street Elementary for his first two years, then finished through sixth grade at David T. Howard Elementary. For secondary school he followed his sister to the Laboratory High School of Atlanta University until it closed after Martin's second year of attendance. In 1942, at age thirteen, he transferred to the only black high school in Atlanta, Booker T. Washington; he graduated in 1944. Throughout his schooling, Martin studied hard; participated in activities, particularly sports; enjoyed his classmates; dated; and wore smart clothes. His love of clothing and fine shoes continued throughout his life, and because of it he was good-naturedly nicknamed "Tweed."

Martin's College Years

At the age of fifteen, Martin matriculated at the same college his father had attended, Morehouse. His years at Morehouse from 1944 to 1948 had a great impact on his development as a speaker, social activist, preacher, and thinker. His teachers at the all-black college expected their students to rise above the hostile and segregated society in which they lived and work to be successful, maintain humanitarian values, and provide leadership for their people. Martin majored in sociology and minored in English. Both subjects served him well later in life: His study of English trained him to be a more cogent and powerful speaker and writer, and his study of sociology led him to understand the political, social, and economic forces that shaped America, especially the connection between economic inequalities and racism.

During the summer months and his college holidays Martin took temporary jobs as a common laborer, despite the fact that his father's influence with successful Atlanta businessmen could have connected him with easier and better paying work. He labored on a tobacco plantation, worked for Atlanta's Railway Express Company unloading trucks, and helped in the stockroom at the Southern Spring Bed Mattress Company. He discovered how blacks received less pay than whites for the same work, how they were given the worst jobs, and how they were trapped in lives with little hope and limited prospects for their families. Perhaps because of these firsthand experiences and the social activism that they inspired, Martin joined the National Association for the Advancement of Colored People (NAACP). Participation in the NAACP and his exposure to various interracial college groups helped to ease Martin's hostility toward white people. After meeting more compassionate whites, Martin began to understand how the destiny of blacks is tied to America's destiny. He formulated a philosophical position that "in the final analysis the white man cannot ignore the Negro problem, because he is part of the Negro and the Negro is part of him. The Negro's agony diminishes the white man, and the Negro's salvation enlarges the white man."

It was also in college that Martin reevaluated an earlier rejection of the ministry. At Morehouse he listened to the eloquent and scholarly preaching of the Reverend Dr. Benjamin Mays and the head of the Theological Department, Dr. George D. Kelsey. Martin learned that the spiritual nature of self can meaningfully be blended with one's intellectual self. At age seventeen, just after he finished his junior year, Martin alerted Daddy King that he felt inspired to join the ministry. Elated, Daddy King suggested that his son deliver a sermon to a small group in an auxiliary room at Ebenezer Church. When the word got out that the young King was going to preach, enough people showed up that the service was moved to the main sanctuary. Martin demonstrated his natural gift for oratory, and the sermon was hugely successful. Martin became very serious about his call to the ministry and his desire to serve.

Crozer Theological Seminary

At age nineteen Martin graduated from Morehouse and accepted a scholarship to Crozer Theological Seminary near Philadelphia, studying there from 1948 to 1951. At Crozer, an integrated school, Martin made many friends, both black and white. He even fell in love with a white girl for a short time and was the first black to be elected student body president.

Martin worked very hard studying ethics, social philosophy, and church history and graduated with a straight-A average in 1951. He was awarded the Pearl Plafker Award as an outstanding student and the J. Lewis Crozer Fellowship for graduate study. At Crozer, Martin was profoundly influenced by the work of theologian Walter Rauschenbusch, whose social ideas helped form Martin's conviction that "any religion which professes to be concerned about the souls of men and is not concerned about the social and economic conditions that scar the soul, is a spiritually moribund religion." The young theological student also embraced the ideas of the influential Indian religious reformer Mahatma Gandhi. Gandhi, who believed that the pathway to social change was through love and peacefulness, had freed India from harsh British rule using the power of nonviolent resistance. In his work *Stride Toward Freedom: The Montgomery Story* Martin wrote, "As the days unfolded . . . the inspiration of Mahatma Gandhi began to exert its influence. I had come to see early that the Christian doctrine of love operating through the Gandhian method of nonviolence was one of the most potent weapons available to the Negro in his struggle for freedom." The tactics of Gandhi and the ethics of Jesus Christ would serve as the guiding forces of Martin's leadership.

In 1951 Martin went to Boston University to earn a Ph.D. There he came in contact with a strong, secure black community. He dated frequently, engaged in philosophical discussions, enjoyed sports, and went with friends to local nightclubs in Boston's black neighborhoods. As his Ph.D. studies progressed, Martin came to the realization that he had a moral obligation to return to the South to help his people rise above poverty and segregation. The South, after all, was his home; the South offered him a sense of place and the blacks there were his people. He wrote once that "despite the existence of Jim Crow which kept reminding us at all times of the color of our skin, we had the feeling that something remarkable was unfolding in the South, and we wanted to be on hand to witness it."

Through a mutual friend, Martin met Coretta Scott, a young woman from Alabama who was training in Boston at the New England Conservatory of Music. The daughter of a successful landowner in Marion, Alabama, Coretta went first to Antioch College in Ohio and then to Boston to pursue a career as a concert soprano. The gifted singer enchanted Martin immediately with her beauty, wit, and intelligence. At the end of their first date together Martin uncharacteristically blurted out, "You have all the qualities that I expect to find in the girl I'd like to have for a wife." They were together constantly, walking, discussing philosophy and life, attending concerts, dancing, and, of course, revealing their feelings and beliefs about the future. Coretta initially resisted Martin's hints at marriage because she was determined to establish her own singing career and because she was leery of the demands of being a minister's wife. Moreover, Daddy King was pressuring Martin to marry a prominent young woman whom Martin had dated in Atlanta. But Martin would not be denied, and Reverend King Sr. performed the marriage ceremony on June 18, 1953. The newlyweds returned to Boston so Martin could complete his Ph.D. residency and Coretta could finish her course work in music.

Montgomery

In January of 1954 the sophisticated congregation of the Dexter Avenue Baptist Church in Montgomery, Alabama, invited Martin to present a trial sermon. They were enthralled with the sincerity and profundity of Martin's thought and offered him the job as pastor. After much consideration the Kings moved to Montgomery. Reflecting back on this point in their lives, Coretta Scott King wrote, "Though I had been opposed to going to Montgomery, I realize now that it was an inevitable part of a greater plan for our lives. Even in 1954 I felt that my husband was being prepared—and I too—for a special role about which we would learn more later." During the next fifteen months, the Kings settled peacefully into their new life in Montgomery. Martin completed his dissertation, he received his Ph.D. from Boston University, and he and his wife Coretta had their first child, Yolanda Denise (Yoki), on November 17, 1955. Within a month of the birth, however, the quiet life of a successful minister came to an end when Rosa Parks was arrested for refusing to give up her seat to a white person on a Montgomery bus.

Rosa Parks's minister, Reverend Ralph Abernathy, asked Martin to join a committee to organize a boycott of the city buses. Several factors made Martin reluctant to take action: He was a new father, he was just settling into his role as a minister, and he had concerns about the resolve of his fellow black ministers to stick with a long and arduous boycott. But Martin acquiesced and initiated the boycott by distributing forty thousand leaflets encouraging blacks to avoid the buses starting on Monday, December 5. That same day Martin was elected as president of the Montgomery Improvement Association (MIA), a newly formed committee to improve all areas of life in which blacks were treated differently than whites. That night he spoke to a huge crowd, telling them that they were protesting in order to give birth to justice and that black people, a great people, have the opportunity to "inject new meaning and dignity into the veins of our civilization." The boycott lasted 381 tumultuous days until November 13, 1956, when the U.S. Supreme Court unanimously upheld a District Court ruling that segregation on Alabama's buses was unconstitutional.

Throughout the boycott Martin and other black leaders held mass meetings to teach and encourage nonviolence. The success of the nonviolent boycott unleashed the rage of the white segregationists, particularly members of the White Citizens Council and the Ku Klux Klan (KKK). Martin's success made him and his family targets of racist behavior. He and Coretta received phone calls at all hours of the night filled with racist slurs and death threats, he was harassed by the police and Montgomery city fathers, he was arrested, and, on January 30, 1956, the King house was bombed. Luckily no one was hurt. Despite the danger, Martin held fast to his stance of nonviolence. After returning to find his home bombed, he calmly told the crowd that had gathered, "I want you to go home and put down your weapons. We cannot solve this problem through retaliatory violence. We must meet violence with nonviolence."

Martin's Call to the Nation

The experiences in Montgomery deepened Martin's commitment to interconnecting spirituality and nonviolence to bring about social reform. To this end he traveled widely preaching, he wrote his first book entitled *Stride Toward Freedom: The Montgomery Story*, and he broadened the base of the civil rights movement by establishing the Southern Christian Leadership Conference (SCLC). Encouraged by the cooperation of the black ministers in Montgomery, as well as sporadic protests in other Southern cities, Martin hoped to focus and mobilize social change efforts using the SCLC as a central organizing body. Approximately one hundred church leaders gathered at Ebenezer Baptist Church in

Atlanta to create this social action arm of the black church. When the SCLC held its first formal meeting in New Orleans on February 14, 1957, Martin was elected its first president. Martin articulated five goals of the SCLC:

> First, to stimulate nonviolent, direct mass action to expose and remove the barriers of segregation and discrimination; second to disseminate the creative philosophy and techniques of nonviolence through local and area workshops; third to secure the right and unhampered use of the ballot for every citizen; fourth to achieve full citizenship rights, and the total integration of the Negro into American life; and fifth, to reduce the cultural lag through our citizenship training program.

One of Martin's first actions was to send a letter to President Eisenhower asking him to initiate a White House conference on civil rights. When their request was denied, Martin and the SCLC organized a Prayer Pilgrimage to be held at the Abraham Lincoln Memorial in Washington, D.C. On May 17, 1957, three years to the day after the *Brown v. Board of Education* decision, Martin, along with Roy Wilkens, the executive secretary of the NAACP, and other black leaders from around the nation, spoke to the largest civil rights crowd in history to date, approximately thirty-seven thousand. In his keynote address, Martin called on both the Democrats and Republicans to support their struggle for freedom, and he appealed to President Eisenhower for legislation to protect blacks' right to vote. The crowd chanted "Give us the ballot." Later President Eisenhower agreed to meet with Martin and a small contingency of black leaders. Despite their discussion about voting rights and the need for police protection from the rising violence against blacks, Eisenhower took no action.

Martin's work load had increased tremendously. He was the president of the Montgomery Improvement Association and the SCLC, he fulfilled numerous public appearances, he wrote prolifically, and he was a busy pastor of Dexter Avenue Baptist Church. Moreover, the Kings had their second child, Martin Luther III, a son born in Montgomery on October 23, 1957. Martin was extremely overworked and the tension was intense. To make matters worse, in 1958 Martin was attacked by a mentally ill woman while autographing his book in a New York department store.

Sit-Ins and Freedom Rides

After Martin recuperated the Kings took a month-long trip to India as guests of Prime Minister Nehru to study Gandhi's techniques of nonviolence. Upon his return to America, Martin knew that he would have to reorganize his life so he could devote more time to the civil rights movement. Consequently he made the difficult decision to resign his position as head minister at Dexter Avenue Baptist Church and join his father as assistant pastor at Ebenezer Baptist Church in Atlanta, the headquarters of SCLC. Violence was mounting throughout the South as many hostile whites expressed outrage toward the changes that blacks were demanding. In response, the SCLC increased its nonviolent protests.

One tactic that proved to be effective was the sit-in. The first sit-in took place in Greensboro, North Carolina, at the Woolworth drug store lunch counter. Four black freshmen from a local college quietly sat down at the all-white counter and ordered lunch. When they were refused service, they sat there all day, impeding Woolworth's lunch business. Martin introduced another protest strategy called selective buying. Dr. King and the SCLC encouraged blacks to avoid purchasing products from businesses that practiced segregation, stating bluntly that it is immoral for blacks to patronize organizations that oppress them.

In 1960 approximately seventy-five students invited Martin to join their sit-in at the segregated lunch counter at Atlanta's largest department store, Rich's. When all were arrested, including Martin, the protest made national headlines. All of the students were eventually released, but Martin was jailed for violating a one-year probation that he had been given for an earlier minor traffic violation. Martin was sentenced to four months of hard labor at Reidsville State Prison. At four thirty in the morning guards at the local jail put Martin in handcuffs and leg irons and took him four hundred miles to Reidsville. Senator John F. Kennedy, who was in a tight presidential race against the Republican Richard Nixon, made a highly publicized telephone call to Coretta, who was five months pregnant with her third child, Dexter Scott, expressing his regrets and his support. Meanwhile, Kennedy's brother, Robert, convinced the county judge to release Dr. King on bail after only one day in prison. This gesture was a shrewd political move on the part of Kennedy who, with the election just one month away, earned, with Martin's support, over 75 percent of the black vote.

Shortly after Kennedy's inauguration in 1961 students from another civil rights group, the Congress of Racial Equality (CORE), supported by the SCLC, initiated the Freedom Rides. Motivated by the U.S. Supreme Court's ruling banning segregation on interstate buses, the Freedom Riders intended to not only test the law but also to check Kennedy's commitment to act on civil rights issues. They informed the Kennedy administration of their intent, and interracial groups of students boarded Greyhound and Trailways buses in Washington, D.C., and headed south to challenge policies of segregated restaurants, rest rooms, and bus stations. Along the way the highly publicized riders met hostility: A bus was burned in Alabama, riders were arrested in Mississippi, and violence exploded in Birmingham and Montgomery. The white mob in Montgomery, numbering approximately one thousand, beat up the riders so viciously that Attorney General Robert F. Kennedy ordered over four hundred federal marshals to restore order. The Freedom Rides pushed the civil rights movement into the remotest areas of the South and helped raise the level of awareness throughout the entire country.

The Albany and Birmingham Campaigns

The next major civil rights confrontation happened in Albany in November 1961 when three young black students were denied service at the city bus terminal dining room. When they refused to leave, they were arrested. Shortly thereafter a group of Freedom Riders arrived in Albany to help local black leaders integrate public facilities, and they too were arrested. Exasperated, black organizers called Martin for help. White city officials acted quickly and had Martin, who was leading a procession of protesters, arrested for obstructing the sidewalk and marching in a parade without a permit. He was jailed for two days. Through the course of the prolonged Albany campaign Martin would be arrested three times. Despite the fact that Martin and others preached nonviolence, the Albany movement turned violent. A large crowd of frustrated and angry blacks blocked the streets and threw rocks and bottles at one hundred Albany police. This time the police did not retaliate; instead they retreated, making very few arrests. The incident was televised nationally and to the TV viewers the incident looked like Martin's pledge of nonviolence had collapsed and things were spiraling out of control. With momentum seemingly on their side, Albany officials secured a federal injunction that outlawed any further demonstrations for ten days.

Albany turned out to be Martin's greatest failure: local leadership was not sharply organized, Martin was successfully portrayed in the media as an outside troublemaker, parts of the campaign had a feel of aggression rather than nonviolence, and the public facilities were not immediately desegregated. Martin also acknowledged that the Albany campaign lacked focus because he and his supporters attempted to overturn segregation in all public facilities rather than concentrating on one or two targets.

The mistakes made in Albany were not repeated in the successful 1963 Birmingham, Alabama, campaign. Martin often referred to Birmingham as the most thoroughly segregated city in America. Blacks were shamefully subjugated in Birmingham: They were discriminated against in employment, able to secure only low-paying menial jobs with no benefits or hope of improved wages; they made up a very small percentage of registered voters, despite constituting over 40 percent of the population; the NAACP was outlawed; and blacks had been repeatedly victimized by racial violence and property damage—several had been murdered by whites who walked away without penalty. Perhaps Birmingham's racial position, particularly on the police force, was best symbolized by the popular commissioner of public safety, Eugene "Bull" Connor, when he demeaned blacks by stating, "If you ask half of them what freedom means, they couldn't tell you." Martin once stated that in "Connor's Birmingham, the silent password was fear. It was a fear not only on the part of the black oppressed, but also in the hearts of the white oppressors. Guilt was a part of their fear." Martin knew that Birmingham would be the centerpiece of the civil rights movement. "If Birmingham could be cracked," he recalled later, "the direction of the entire nonviolent movement in the South could take a significant turn. It was our faith that 'as Birmingham goes, so goes the South.'"

In the summer of 1962 Martin, the SCLC, Birmingham church leaders, and Reverend Fred Shuttlesworth, Birmingham's foremost freedom fighter, whose house had recently been dynamited by racists, planned Operation "C," signifying confrontation. Operation "C" had a clear goal: the desegregation of restaurants and easier access to better jobs for blacks. Volunteer leaders were trained in nonviolent tactics that stressed that fighting the Birmingham police would be playing into the authorities' hands. At first the sit-ins, demonstrations, and boycotts of Birmingham businesses went without incident. However, on April 7, 1963, the police broke loose and charged into a crowd of demonstrators, beating them with sticks and unleashing police dogs. In response, on April 12, Martin and Ralph Abernathy led a large crowd toward central Birmingham singing the movement's rallying song *We Shall Overcome*. This march stood out in Martin's mind: "All along the way Negroes lined the streets. We were singing, and they were joining in. Occasionally the singing from the sidewalks was interspersed with applause. As we neared the downtown area, Bull Connor ordered his men to arrest us. Ralph and I were hauled off by two muscular policemen, clutching the backs of our shirts in handfuls." Over fifty protesters were taken to jail and Martin was placed in solitary confinement and denied the right to make a telephone call for over twenty-four hours. During his eight days in jail, Martin composed "Letter from Birmingham Jail," one of the most insightful statements of the civil rights movement. Immediately upon his release, Martin and Ralph Abernathy drew up plans for the next phase of the Birmingham strategy, a children's crusade for freedom. On May 2, 1963, over a thousand black schoolchildren, ranging in age from six to eighteen, marched toward downtown singing freedom songs. Again Bull Connor unleashed the police, who used dogs and fire hoses to break up the crowd and arrest hundreds of young people. The images of nonviolent children attacked by police dogs and violently swept off their feet with surging water streams shocked the viewing public and resulted in a national outcry of protest.

The reaction in Washington, D.C., was so overwhelming that President Kennedy was compelled to send a delegated representative and three thousand federal troops to Birmingham to force a settlement. On May 10, Birmingham officials agreed to desegregate city facilities and drop the charges against demonstrators who had been arrested. Enraged and frustrated, hard-core white segregationists turned once more to violence by bombing the Birmingham headquarters of the SCLC and the house of Martin's brother, A.D. King. Tensions cooled somewhat when President Kennedy publicly supported the Birmingham crusade, and just three weeks later he asked Congress to enact a comprehensive Civil Rights Bill. The segregated South would never be the same again.

The March on Washington

Late in the summer of 1963 Martin organized his Lincoln Memorial Prayer Pilgrimage in Washington, D.C., a site chosen for its symbolic meaning. This demonstration, called the March on Washington for Jobs and Freedom, generated an outpouring of support, far outstripping the 1957 rally at the same site. On August 28 an estimated 250,000 people, both black and white, came to Washington from across the nation. Following numerous speakers, Martin stepped to the podium as the keynote speaker and delivered his address outlining his dream for America. Martin's "I Have a Dream" speech touched the national conscience by portraying an America where "all of God's children, black men and white men, Jews and Gentiles, Protestants and Catholics, will be able to join hands and sing in the words of the old Negro spiritual, 'Free at last! Free at last! Great God Almighty, we are free at last!'" Coretta wrote that these last words drifted out onto an awed silence and then the crowd broke, "They kept on shouting in one thunderous voice, and for that brief moment the Kingdom of God seemed to have come to earth." Three months later, however, darkness descended when President John F. Kennedy, the nation's most potent voice for human rights, was assassinated in Dallas.

The January 4, 1964, issue of *Time* magazine named Martin Luther King Jr. "Man of the Year" for 1963, making Martin the first black American to receive the honor. Just two months after the *Time* accolade, the House of Representatives, urged on by the new presi-

Martin Luther King Jr. speaks to a crowd in Selma, Alabama, in 1965. His rousing speeches helped to ignite the civil rights movement.

dent, Lyndon B. Johnson, passed the Civil Rights Bill and sent it on to the Senate. After eighty-three days of heated debate, the bill ultimately won approval and was signed by President Johnson on July 2. The 1964 Civil Rights Act guaranteed blacks the right to vote, banned discrimination in all organizations that received money from the government, and provided blacks full access to public facilities.

Martin's stature as an inspirational leader was celebrated in October 1964 when Martin, at age thirty-five, was chosen to receive the coveted Nobel Peace Prize. He was awarded the prize in Oslo, Norway, for his struggle for freedom and his adherence to nonviolence.

Despite Martin's honors and some encouraging signs of positive change in government, the summer of 1964 revealed an entrenched racist meanness in the nation. The SCLC launched a Southern offensive to get blacks to register to vote. Martin selected Selma, Alabama, as a target for voter registration because it was at the heart of the state's black-belt counties where very few blacks voted; in fact, in some counties not a single black voter was even registered. In Selma only one in fifty blacks actually voted. One of Martin's goals was to pressure President Johnson to enact legislation to protect the rights of blacks to vote and to provide federal inspectors to guarantee that they were not threatened during the voter registration process.

Selma

With the advance of federal desegregation, white citizens of Selma organized a White Citizen's Council to coordinate efforts to keep blacks from obtaining power and rights. Many of the efforts of this council were overseen by a tough county sheriff, James Clark. In January 1965 Martin orchestrated imposing demonstrations protesting voter registration practices in Selma.

Five hundred blacks marched to the county courthouse to register, but police maneuvered them into an out-of-the-way, roped-off area in an alley. Despite waiting there all day, none were registered. These humiliating stall tactics lasted for approximately two weeks; each day James Clark and his officers arrested anyone who protested the procedure. When a federal order was issued to prevent voter harassment, city officials admitted only one registrant at a time, requiring each one to spend a lengthy amount of time completing useless and unfair forms and questionnaires.

Again, Martin was arrested, this time for leading an illegal parade. Frustrated, more than 250 protesters locked arms outside the courthouse and sang songs, joined later by 500 children who left school to participate. An angry James Clark had the adults arrested and the children charged with juvenile delinquency. This predictable overreaction by racist authorities attracted a great deal of publicity, which eventually reaped benefits when the U.S. Department of Justice decreed that the Selma registration process must be discarded and a minimum of 100 registrants must be processed a day. This victory spread throughout Alabama as more and more blacks demanded their right to register. In hopes of emphasizing the importance of voter registration, Martin planned a march from Selma to Montgomery. Alabama's governor, George Wallace, promptly banned the march, but undeterred, 500 protesters led by Martin's close associate, Hosea Williams, marched in defiance of the order. Just outside of Selma the road was blocked by state troopers who told them to disperse and go back to their churches. Quietly, following their nonviolent tactics, the marchers knelt down. While white spectators cheered them on, the troopers charged, brutally beating and seriously injuring many of the kneeling marchers with clubs, bullwhips, cattle prods, and tear gas. The news of the horrific event spread, labeled by the media as "Bloody Sunday." Shocked, but not intimidated, Martin made plans for another Selma to Montgomery march.

Two weeks after Bloody Sunday, Martin led a group of three thousand blacks and whites down the same road as the earlier march. At the outset, Martin told the protesters, "I can't promise that you won't get beaten; I can't promise you won't get your house bombed; I can't promise that you won't get scarred up a bit, but we must stand up for what is right." The march was orderly, peaceful, and uneventful. The police did not attack, and Martin, after a prayer session on the highway, quietly asked the marchers to return to Selma. The march had been somewhat of a compromise, each side seeming to score a victory: The protesters established their right to march, and the authorities turned them back. Perhaps things would have ended there, but a foolish, hateful act stirred the animosities once again. That night a white Unitarian minister, James Reeb, ate dinner with two other clergymen at a black-owned restaurant and, as they were leaving, four Klansmen attacked them, shouting, "White niggers!" and crushed Reeb's skull with a wooden club. He died a short time later.

Reports of the Reeb killing, added with the appalling news footage of Bloody Sunday, horrified much of the nation. President Johnson finally broke his silence and addressed a joint congressional session. Broadcast on national television, Johnson concluded that "what happened in Selma is part of a far larger movement which reaches into every section and state of America. It is the effort of American Negroes to secure for themselves the full blessings of American life. . . . Their cause must be our cause, too. Because it is not just Negroes but really all of us, who must overcome the crippling legacy of bigotry and injustice. And we shall overcome!" Martin and the freedom fighters were encouraged and gratified by the president's message. Later that year, President Johnson signed the 1965 Voting Rights Act, which barred literacy tests as a registration requirement and allowed federal authorities to intervene when the right to vote was obstructed.

The Freedom Movement Pushes into the North

Martin knew that the freedom struggle was not confined to the South. This was emphatically punctuated during the summer of 1965, when violent riots exploded in Watts, a black ghetto of Los Angeles, resulting in over thirty-five hundred arrests and thirty-five deaths. At a Baltimore meeting of the SCLC Martin decided to push his campaign to selected northern cities in order to fight poverty, inadequate housing, and unemployment. Martin understood that to simply calm the rioting was not enough; real social and political change for equality had to take place or violence would erupt over and over again.

Early in 1966 Martin established an SCLC office in Chicago and the King family, in order to understand the daily life of the downtrodden, moved into a dingy little tenement apartment in a Chicago ghetto. Immediately Martin and workers for the SCLC began to organize the neighbors, explaining that they could unify as renters to demand housing improvements. Martin wanted the poor to understand that even they could exercise legal and legitimate power. In the summer of 1966 Martin led a rally, named "Freedom Sunday," of over fifty thousand people at Soldier Field demanding better housing, jobs, city services, and schools. Tensions rose quickly: Some whites felt that Martin's activities, though nonviolent, would ultimately generate violence; and militant black leaders wanted more aggressive leadership. Two black youths were killed in rioting on

Chicago's West Side, and the governor of Illinois mobilized the national guard to maintain order.

Since substantive changes had not been made, Martin feared that the summer of 1967 would be even more violent than 1966. As early as June 2 riots broke out in Boston where more than sixty people were injured. Before the summer ended, over thirty riots exploded across America, including Detroit, where forty-three died and over three hundred were seriously injured. Martin preached that the boiling unrest could only be eased if the oppressive yoke of poverty was lifted. By the end of 1967 Martin had announced a new initiative, the Poor People's Campaign, dedicated to eradicating poverty through the development of meaningful employment for people of all colors.

Martin's Death

Martin's work on the Poor People's Campaign was interrupted when the sanitation workers in Memphis, Tennessee, went on strike for better wages and working conditions. Martin's first demonstration in Memphis to support the striking workers turned violent and one black person was killed. Chagrined at the violent result of the first demonstration, Martin returned on April 3, 1968, to try another march, one rooted in nonviolence.

The very next day, April 4, 1968, after a successful meeting with his staff, Martin retired to his room at the Lorraine Motel in Memphis. Shortly before six, while standing pensively on his balcony, a gunshot fired by an escaped convict named James Earl Ray mortally wounded Martin in the neck. He died an hour later at Memphis's St. Joseph's Hospital. People across the nation were shocked at Martin's brutal and senseless slaying. Upon his death riots broke out in over a hundred American cities; thousands were injured, almost fifty were killed, and over twenty thousand were arrested.

Grief, shock, and introspective questions were articulated by millions around the world. The fact that the archetype of nonviolence should meet such a violent end dramatized the very anger in American society that Martin had tirelessly struggled against. He once wrote, "The oceans of history are made turbulent by the ever-rising tides of hate. History is cluttered with the wreckage of nations and individuals that pursued that self-defeating path of hate. Love is the key to the solution of the problems of the world." Martin's campaign to free blacks and help the poor was built on love without egotism and selflessness without pride.

The Philosophy of Nonviolence

Martin Luther King Jr.

In 1955, the black seamstress Rosa Parks refused to relinquish her seat to a white passenger on a Montgomery city bus. The Montgomery bus boycott that ensued not only desegregated city buses, it also catapulted Martin Luther King Jr.—the leader of the boycott—to national prominence and gave rise to nonviolent social protest as a guiding principle in the struggle for civil rights. The following excerpt from *Stride Toward Freedom*, King's autobiographical account of the Montgomery bus boycott, perhaps best describes the basic tenets of the philosophy of nonviolence. Central to this civil rights approach is the principle of love, writes King, who emphatically believed that "someone must have sense enough and morality enough to cut off the chain of hate."

❦ ❦ ❦

When I went to Montgomery as a pastor, I had not the slightest idea that I would later become involved in a crisis in which nonviolent resistance would be applicable. I neither started the protest nor suggested it. I simply responded to the call of the people for a spokesman. When the protest began, my mind, consciously or unconsciously, was driven back to the Sermon on the Mount, with its sublime teachings on love, and the Gandhian method of nonviolent resistance. As the days unfolded, I came to see the power of nonviolence more and more. Living through the actual experience of the protest, nonviolence became more than a method to which I gave intellectual assent; it became a commitment to a way of life. Many of the things that I had not cleared up intellectually concerning nonviolence were now solved in the sphere of practical action.

Nonviolence as a Philosophy

Since the philosophy of nonviolence played such a positive role in the Montgomery Movement, it may be wise to turn to a brief discussion of some basic aspects of this philosophy.

First, it must be emphasized that nonviolent resistance is not a method for cowards; it does resist. If one uses this method because he is afraid or merely because he lacks the instruments of violence, he is not truly nonviolent. This is why Gandhi often said that if cowardice is the only alternative to violence, it is better to fight. He made this statement conscious of the fact that there is always another alternative: no individual or group need submit to any wrong, nor need they use violence to right the wrong; there is the way of nonviolence resistance. This is ultimately the way of the strong man. It is not a method of stagnant passivity. The phrase "passive resistance" often gives the false impression that this is a short of "do-nothing method" in which the resister quietly and passively accepts evil. But nothing is further from the truth. For while the nonviolent resister is passive in the sense that he is not physically aggressive toward his opponent, his mind and emotions are always active, constantly seeking to persuade his opponent that he is wrong. The method is passive physically, but strongly active spiritually. It is not passive nonresistance to evil, it is active nonviolent resistance to evil.

A second basic fact that characterizes nonviolence is that it does not seek to defeat or humiliate the opponent, but to win his friendship and understanding. The nonviolent resister must often express his protest through noncoöperation or boycotts, but he realizes that these are not ends themselves; they are merely means to awaken a sense of moral shame in the opponent. The end is redemption and reconciliation. The aftermath of nonviolence is the creation of the beloved community, while the aftermath of violence is tragic bitterness.

A third characteristic of this method is that the attack is directed against forces of evil rather than against persons who happen to be doing the evil. It is evil that the nonviolent resister seeks to defeat, not the persons victimized by evil. If he is opposing racial injustice, the nonviolent resister has the vision to see that the basic tension is not between races. As I like to say to the people in Montgomery: "The tension in this city is not between white people and Negro people. The tension is, at bottom, between justice and injustice, between the forces of light and the forces of darkness. And if there is a victory, it will be a victory not merely for fifty thousand Negroes, but a victory for justice and the forces of light. We are out to defeat injustice and not white persons who may be unjust."

A fourth point that characterizes nonviolent resistance is a willingness to accept suffering without retaliation, to accept blows from the opponent without striking back. "Rivers of blood may have to flow before we gain our freedom, but it must be our blood," Gandhi said to his countrymen. The nonviolent resister is willing to accept violence if necessary, but never to inflict it. He does not seek to dodge jail. If going to jail is necessary, he enters it "as a bridegroom enters the bride's chamber."

One may well ask: "What is the nonviolent resister's justification for this ordeal to which he invites men, for this mass political application of the ancient doctrine of turning the other cheek?" The answer is found in the realization that unearned suffering is redemptive. Suffering, the nonviolent resister realizes, has tremendous educational and transforming possibilities. "Things of fundamental importance to people are not secured by reason alone, but have to be purchased with their suffering," said Gandhi. He continues: "Suffering is infinitely more powerful than the law of the jungle for converting the opponent and opening his ears which are otherwise shut to the voice of reason."

A fifth point concerning nonviolent resistance is that it avoids not only external physical violence but also internal violence of spirit. The nonviolent resister not only refuses to shoot his opponent but he also refuses to hate him. At the center of nonviolence stands the principle of love. The nonviolent resister would contend that in the struggle for human dignity, the oppressed people of the world must not succumb to the temptation of becoming bitter or indulging in hate campaigns. To retaliate in kind would do nothing but intensify the existence of hate in the universe. Along the way of life, someone must have sense enough and morality enough to cut off the chain of hate. This can only be done by projecting the ethic of love to the center of our lives.

The Meaning of Love

In speaking of love at this point, we are not referring to some sentimental or affectionate emotion. It would be nonsense to urge men to love their oppressors in an affectionate sense. Love in this connection means understanding, redemptive good will. Here the Greek language comes to our aid. There are three words for love in the Greek New Testament. First, there is *eros*. In Platonic philosophy *eros* meant the yearning of the soul for the realm of the divine. It has come now to mean a sort of aesthetic or romantic love. Second, there is *philia* which means intimate affection between personal friends. *Philia* denotes a sort of reciprocal love; the person loves because he is loved. When we speak of loving those who oppose us, we refer to neither *eros* nor *philia*; we speak of a love which is expressed in the Greek word *agape*. *Agape* means understanding, redeeming good will for all men. It is an overflowing love which is purely spontaneous, unmotivated, groundless, and creative. It is not set in motion by any quality or function of its object. It is the love of God operating in the human heart.

Agape is disinterested love. It is a love in which the individual seeks not his own good, but the good of his neighbor (I Cor. 10:24). *Agape* does not begin by discriminating between worthy and unworthy people, or any qualities people possess. It begins by loving others *for their sakes*. It is an entirely "neighbor-regarding concern for others," which discovers the neighbor in every man it meets. Therefore, *agape* makes no distinction between friend and enemy; it is directed toward both. If one loves an individual merely on account of his friendliness, he loves him for the sake of the benefits to be gained from the friendship, rather than for the friend's own sake. Consequently, the best way to assure oneself that Love is disinterested is to have love for the enemy-neighbor from whom you can expect no good in return, but only hostility and persecution.

Another basic point about *agape* is that it springs from the *need* of the other person—his need for belonging to the best in the human family. The Samaritan who helped the Jew on the Jericho Road was "good" because he responded to the human need that he was presented with. God's love is eternal and fails not because man needs his love. St. Paul assures us that the loving act of redemption was done "while we were yet sinners"—that is, at the point of our greatest need for love. Since the white man's personality is greatly distorted by segregation, and his soul is greatly scarred, he needs the love of the Negro. The Negro must love the white man, because the white man needs his love to remove his tensions, insecurities, and fears.

Love in Action

Agape is not a weak, passive love. It is love in action. *Agape* is love seeking to preserve and create community. It is insistence on community even when one seeks to break it. *Agape* is a willingness to sacrifice in the interest of mutuality. *Agape* is a willingness to go to any length to restore community. It doesn't stop at the first mile, but it goes the second mile to restore community. It is a willingness to forgive, not seven times, but seventy times seven to restore community. The cross is the eternal expression of the length to which God will go in order to restore broken community. The resurrection is a symbol of God's triumph over all the forces that seek to block community. The Holy Spirit is the continuing community creating reality that moves through history. He who works against community is working against the whole of creation. Therefore, if I respond to hate with a reciprocal hate I do nothing but intensify the cleavage in broken community. I can only close the gap in broken community by meeting hate with love. If I meet hate with hate, I become depersonalized, because creation is so designed that my personality can only be fulfilled in the context of community. Booker T. Washington was right: "Let no man pull you so low as to make you hate him." When he pulls you that low he brings you to the point of working against community; he drags you to the point of defying creation, and thereby becoming depersonalized.

In the final analysis, *agape* means a recognition of the fact that all life is interrelated. All humanity is involved in a single process, and all men are brothers. To the degree that I harm my brother, no matter what he is doing to me, to that extent I am harming myself. For example, white men often refuse federal aid to education in order to avoid giving the Negro his rights; but because all men are brothers they cannot deny Negro children without harming their own. They end, all efforts to the contrary, by hurting themselves. Why is this? Because men are brothers. If you harm me, you harm yourself.

Love, *agape*, is the only cement that can hold this broken community together. When I am commanded to love, I am commanded to restore community, to resist injustice, and to meet the needs of my brothers.

Faith in the Future

A sixth basic fact about nonviolent resistance is that it is based on the conviction that the universe is on the side of justice. Consequently, the believer in nonviolence has deep faith in the future. This faith is another reason why the nonviolent resister can accept suffering without retaliation. For he knows that in his struggle for justice he has cosmic companionship. It is true that there are devout believers in nonviolence who find it difficult to believe in a personal God. But even these persons believe in the existence of some creative force that works for universal wholeness. Whether we call it an unconscious process, an impersonal Brahman, or a Personal Being of matchless power and infinite love, there is a creative force in this universe that works to bring the disconnected aspects of reality into a harmonious whole.

The Role of Martin Luther King Jr.

August Meier

In his crusade for black rights, Martin Luther King Jr. occupied a strategically important position at the vital center of the movement—between black radicalism and black conservatism, as well as between blacks and whites. In the following article, written three years before King's death, August Meier describes how King's centrist position enabled him to attract large numbers of supporters from mainstream America, noting that his leadership was more symbolic than substantive. King's most important function, Meier writes, was to effectively communicate black woes and aspirations to the white community, while at the same time making direct action protest a respectable means of addressing these concerns. In short, King's presence in the American civil rights movement was invaluable to its success. August Meier is the author of *Negro Thought in America, 1880–1915*, *Negro Protest Thought in the Twentieth Century*, and *A Short History of the American Negro*.

🜚 🜚 🜚

August Meier, "On the Role of Martin Luther King," *New Politics*, vol. 4, Winter 1965, pp. 52–59. Copyright © 1965 by New Politics Publishing Co. Reproduced by permission.

The phenomenon that is Martin Luther King consists of a number of striking paradoxes. The Nobel Prize winner is accepted by the outside world as *the* leader of the nonviolent direct action movement, but he is criticized by many activists within the movement. He is criticized for what appears, at times, as indecisiveness, and more often denounced for a tendency to accept compromise. Yet, in the eyes of most Americans, both black and white, he remains the symbol of militant direct action. So potent is this symbol of King as direct actionist, that a new myth is arising about his historic role. The real credit for developing and projecting the techniques and philosophy of nonviolent direct action in the civil rights arena must be given to the Congress of Racial Equality [CORE] which was founded in 1942, more than a dozen years before the Montgomery bus boycott projected King into international fame. And the idea of mass action by Negroes themselves to secure redress of their grievances must, in large part, be ascribed to the vision of A. Philip Randolph, architect of the March on Washington Movement during World War II. Yet, as we were told in Montgomery on March 25, 1965, King and his followers now assert, apparently without serious contradiction, that a new type of civil rights strategy was born at Montgomery in 1955 under King's auspices.

In a movement in which respect is accorded in direct proportion to the number of times one has been arrested, King appears to keep the number of times he goes to jail to a minimum. In a movement in which successful leaders are those who share in the hardships of their followers, in the risks they take, in the beatings they receive, in the length of time they spend in jail, King tends to leave prison for other important engagements, rather than remaining there and suffering with his followers. In a movement in which leadership ordinarily devolves upon persons who mix democratically with their followers, King remains isolated and aloof. In a movement which prides itself on militancy and "no compromise" with racial discrimination or with the white "power structure," King maintains close relationships with, and appears to be influenced by, Democratic presidents and their emissaries, seems amenable to compromises considered by some half a loaf or less, and often appears willing to postpone or avoid a direct confrontation in the streets.

King's career has been characterized by failures that, in the larger sense, must be accounted triumphs. The buses in Montgomery were desegregated only after lengthy judicial proceedings conducted by the NAACP Legal Defense Fund secured a favorable decision from the U.S. Supreme Court. Nevertheless, the events in Montgomery were a triumph for direct action, and gave this tactic a popularity unknown when identified solely with CORE. King's subsequent major campaigns—in Albany, Georgia; in Danville, Virginia; in Birmingham, Alabama; and in St. Augustine, Florida—ended as failures or with only token accomplishments in those cities. But each of them, chiefly because of his presence, dramatically focused national and international attention on the plight of the Southern Negro, thereby facilitating overall progress. In Birmingham, in particular, demonstrations which fell short of their local goals were directly responsible for a major Federal Civil Rights Act. Essentially, this pattern of local failure and national victory was recently enacted at Selma, Alabama.

King is ideologically committed to disobeying unjust laws and court orders, its the Gandhian tradition, but generally he follows a policy of not disobeying Federal Court orders. In his recent Montgomery speech, he expressed a crude, neo-Marxist interpretation of history romanticizing the Populist movement as a genuine union of black and white common people, ascribing race prejudice to capitalists playing white workers against black. Yet, in practice, he is amenable to compromise with the white bourgeois political and economic Establishment. More important, King enunciates a superficial and eclectic philosophy and by virtue of it he has profoundly awakened the moral conscience of America.

In short, King can be described as a "Conservative Militant."

Militancy and Conservatism

In this combination of militancy with conservatism and caution, of righteousness with respectability, lies the secret of King's enormous success.

Certain important civil rights leaders have dismissed King's position as the product of publicity generated by the mass communications media. But this can be said of the successes of the civil rights nonviolent action movement generally. Without publicity it is hard to conceive that much progress would have been made. In fact, contrary to the official nonviolent direct action philosophy, demonstrations have secured their results not by changing the hearts of the oppressors through a display of nonviolent love, but through the national and international pressures generated by the publicity arising from mass arrests and incidents of violence. And no one has employed this strategy of securing publicity through mass arrests and precipitating violence from white hoodlums and law enforcement officers more than King himself. King abhors violence; as at Selma, for example, he constantly retreats from situations that might result in the deaths of his followers. But he is precisely most successful when, contrary to his deepest wishes, his demonstrations precipitate violence from Southern whites against Negro and white demonstrators. We need only cite Birmingham and Selma to illustrate this point.

Publicity alone does not explain the durability of King's image, or why he remains for the rank and file of whites and blacks alike, the symbol of the direct action movement, the nearest thing to a charismatic leader that the civil rights movement has ever had. At the heart of King's continuing influence and popularity are two facts. First, better than anyone else, he articulates the aspirations of Negroes who respond to the cadence of his addresses, his religious phraseology and manner of speaking, and the vision of his dream for them and for America. King has intuitively adopted the style of the old fashioned Negro Baptist preacher and transformed it into a new art form; he has, indeed, restored oratory to its place among the arts. Second, he communicates Negro aspirations to white America more effectively than anyone else. His religious terminology and manipulation of the Christian symbols of love and non-resistance are partly responsible for his appeal among whites. To talk in terms of Christianity, love, nonviolence is reassuring to the mentality of white America. At the same time, the very superficialities of his philosophy—that rich and eclectic amalgam of Jesus, Hegel, Gandhi and others as outlined in his *Stride Toward Freedom*—makes him appear intellectually profound to the superficially educated middle class white American. Actually, if he were a truly profound religious thinker, like Tillich or Niebuhr, his influence would of necessity be limited to a select audience. But by uttering moral cliches, the Christian pieties, in a magnificent display of oratory, King becomes enormously effective.

King and White Society

If his success with Negroes is largely due to the style of his utterance, his success with whites is a much more complicated matter. For one thing, he unerringly knows how to exploit to maximum effectiveness their growing feeling of guilt. King, of course, is not unique in attaining fame and popularity among whites through playing upon their guilt feelings. James Baldwin is the most conspicuous example of a man who has achieved success with this formula. The incredible fascination which the Black Muslims have for white people, and the posthumous near-sanctification of Malcolm X by many naive whites (in addition to many Negroes whose motivations are, of course, very different), must in large part be attributed to the same source. But King goes beyond this. With intuitive, but extraordinary skill, he not only castigates whites for their sins but, in contrast to angry young writers like Baldwin, he explicitly states his belief in their salvation. Not only will direct action bring fulfillment of the "American Dream" to Negroes but the Negroes' use of direct action will help whites to live up to their Christian and democratic values; it will purify, cleanse and heal the sickness in white society. Whites will benefit as well as Negroes. He has faith that the white man will redeem himself. Negroes must not hate whites, but love them. In this manner, King first arouses the guilt feelings of whites, and then relieves them—though always leaving the lingering feeling in his white listeners that they should support his nonviolent crusade. Like a Greek tragedy, King's performance provides an extraordinary catharsis for the white listener.

King thus gives white men the feeling that he is their good friend, that he poses no threat to them. It is interesting to note that this was the same feeling white men received from Booker T. Washington, the noted early 20th Century accommodator. Both men stressed their faith in the white man; both expressed the belief that the white man could be brought to accord Negroes their rights. Both stressed the importance of whites recognizing the rights of Negroes for the moral health and well-being of white society. Like King, Washington had an extraordinary following among whites. Like King, Washington symbolized for most whites the whole program of Negro advancement. While there are important similarities in the functioning of both men vis-a-vis the community, needless to say, in most respects, their philosophies are in disagreement.

It is not surprising, therefore, to find that King is the recipient of contributions from organizations and individuals who fail to eradicate evidence of prejudice in their own backyards. For example, certain liberal trade union leaders who are philosophically committed to full racial equality, who feel the need to identify their organizations with the cause of militant civil rights, although they are unable to defeat racist elements in their unions, contribute hundreds of thousands of dollars to King's Southern Christian Leadership Conference (SCLC). One might attribute this phenomenon to the fact that SCLC works in the South rather than the North, but this is true also for SNCC [Student Nonviolent Coordinating Committee] which does not benefit similarly from union treasuries. And the fact is that ever since the college students started their sit-ins in 1960, it is SNCC which has been the real spearhead of direct action in most of the South, and has performed the lion's share of work in local communities, while SCLC has received most of the publicity and most of the money. However, while King provides a verbal catharsis for whites, leaving them feeling purified and comfortable, SNCC's uncompromising militancy makes whites feel less comfortable and less beneficent. . . .

King's very tendencies toward compromise and caution, his willingness to negotiate and bargain with White House emissaries, his hesitancy to risk the precipitation of mass violence upon demonstrators, further endear him to whites. He appears to them a "responsible" and "moderate" man. To militant activists, King's failure to march past the State Police on that famous Tuesday morning outside Selma indicated either a lack of courage, or a desire to advance himself by currying Presidential favor. But King's shrinking from a possible bloodbath, his accession to the entreaties of the political Establishment, his acceptance of face-saving compromise in this, as in other instances, are fundamental to the particular role he is playing, and essential for achieving and sustaining his image as a leader of heroic moral stature in the eyes of white men. His caution and compromise keep open the channels of communication between the activists and the majority of the white community. In brief: King makes the nonviolent direct action movement respectable.

Of course, many, if not most, activists reject the notion that the movement should be made respectable. Yet, American history shows that for any reform movement to succeed, it must attain respectability. It must attract moderates, even conservatives, to its ranks. The March on Washington made direct action respectable; Selma made it fashionable. More than any other force, it is Martin Luther King who impressed the civil rights revolution on the American conscience and is attracting that great middle body of American public opinion to its support. It is this revolution of conscience that will undoubtedly lead fairly soon to the elimination of all violations of Negroes' constitutional rights, thereby creating the conditions for the economic and social changes that are necessary if we are to achieve full racial equality. This is not to deny the dangers to the civil rights movement in becoming respectable. Respectability, for example, encourages the attempts of political machines to capture civil rights organizations. Respectability can also become an end in itself, thereby dulling the cutting edge of its protest activities. Indeed, the history of the labor movement reveals how attaining respectability can produce loss of original purpose and character. These perils, however, do not contradict the importance of achieving respectability—even a degree of modishness—if racial equality is ever to be realized.

There is another side to the picture: King would be neither respected nor respectable if there were not more militant activists on his left, engaged in more radical forms of direct action. Without CORE and, especially, SNCC, King would appear "radical" and "irresponsible" rather than "moderate" and "respectable."

King's Centrist Position

King occupies a position of strategic importance as the "vital center" within the civil rights movement. Though he has lieutenants who are far more militant and "radical" than he is, SCLC acts, in effect, as the most cautious, deliberate and "conservative" of the direct action groups because of King's leadership. This permits King and the SCLC to function—almost certainly unintentionally—not only as an organ of communication with the Establishment and majority white public opinion, but as something of a bridge between the activist and more traditionalist or "conservative" civil rights groups, as well. For example, it appears unlikely that the Urban League and NAACP, which supplied most of the funds, would have participated in the 1963 March on Washington if King had not done so. Because King agreed to go along with SNCC and CORE, the NAACP found it mandatory to join if it was to maintain its image as a protest organization. King's identification with the March was also essential for securing the support of large numbers of white clergymen and their moderate followers. The March was the brainchild of the civil rights movement's ablest strategist and tactician, Bayard Rustin, and the call was issued by A. Philip Randolph.

But it would have been a minor episode in the history of the civil rights movement without King's support.

Yet curiously enough, despite his charisma and international reputation, King thus far has been more a symbol than a power in the civil rights movement. Indeed his strength in the movement has derived less from an organizational base than from his symbolic role. Seven or eight years ago, one might have expected King to achieve an organizationally dominant position in the civil rights movement, at least in its direct action wing. The fact is that in the period after the Montgomery bus boycott, King developed no program and, it is generally agreed, revealed himself as an ineffective administrator who failed to capitalize upon his popularity among Negroes. In 1957, he founded SCLC to coordinate the work of direct action groups that had sprung up in Southern cities. Composed of autonomous units, usually led by Baptist ministers, SCLC does not appear to have developed an overall sense of direction or a program of real breadth and scope. Although the leaders of SCLC affiliates became the race leaders in their communities—displacing the established local conservative leadership of teachers, old-line ministers, businessmen—it is hard for an observer (who admittedly has not been close to SCLC) to perceive exactly what SCLC did before the 1960's except to advance the image and personality of King. King appeared not to direct but to float with the tide of militant direct action. For example, King did not supply the initiative for the bus boycott in Montgomery, but was pushed into the leadership by others, as he himself records in *Stride Toward Freedom*. . . .

King's Strength

Major dailies like the *New York Times* and the *Washington Post*, basically sympathetic to civil rights and racial equality, though more gradualist than the activist organizations, have congratulated the nation upon its good fortune in having a "responsible and moderate" leader like King at the head of the nonviolent action movement (though they overestimate his power and underestimate the symbolic nature of his role). It would be more appropriate to congratulate the civil rights movement for *its* good fortune in having as its symbolic leader a man like King. The fact that he has more prestige than power; the fact that he not only criticizes whites but explicitly believes in their redemption; his ability to arouse creative tension combined with his inclination to shrink from carrying demonstrations to the point where major bloodshed might result; the intellectual simplicity of his philosophy; his tendency to compromise and exert caution, even his seeming indecisiveness on some occasions; the sparing use he makes of going to or staying in jail himself; his friendship with the man in the White House—all are essential to the role he plays, and invaluable for the success of the movement. It is well, of course, that not all civil rights leaders are cut of the same cloth—that King is unique among them. Like Randolph, who functions very differently, King is really an institution. His most important function, I believe, is that of effectively communicating Negro aspirations to white people, of making nonviolent direct action respectable in the eyes of the white majority. In addition, he functions within the movement by occupying a vital center position between its "conservative" and "radical" wings, by symbolizing direct action and attracting people to participate in it without dominating either the civil rights movement or its activist wing. Viewed in this context, traits that many activists criticize in King actually function not as sources of weakness, but as the foundations of his strength.

Profiles · in · History

Malcolm X

The Life and Legacy of Malcolm X

James H. Cone

As the sixties progressed, many African Americans became frustrated with the slow pace of the civil rights movement—and the often vehement backlash that accompanied even limited gains. Into this heated political climate stepped Malcolm X. Promoting the concept of black pride and black nationalism, Malcolm X offered his followers a powerful alternative to Martin Luther King Jr.'s philosophy of passive resistance that had characterized the movement thus far. His fiery speech and militant views galvanized thousands of disillusioned blacks, though many regarded his ideas—he did not rule out the use of violence, for example—extreme and even dangerous. In the following selection, Malcolm X scholar James H. Cone describes the life and impact of Malcolm X, who, despite a miserable early life, went on to transform himself into one of the most influential figures in American history. Cone concludes that Malcolm's greatest legacy is that his exhortations to African Americans to "wake up to their humanity, to their own worth, and to their cultural heritage" continue to empower people today. Cone is the author of *Martin and Malcolm and America: A Dream or a Nightmare?*

James H. Cone, "Malcolm X: The Impact of a Cultural Revolutionary," *The Christian Century*, vol. 109, December 23, 1992, pp. 1,189–94. Copyright © 1992 by the Christian Century Foundation. Reproduced by permission.

🐾 🐾 🐾

No one had a greater impact on the cultural consciousness of African-Americans during the second half of the 20th century than Malcolm X. More than anyone else he revolutionized the black mind, transforming docile Negroes and self-effacing colored people into proud blacks and self-confident African-Americans. Civil rights activists became Black Power militants and declared, "It's nation time." Preachers and religious scholars created a black theology and proclaimed God as liberator and Jesus Christ as black. College and university students demanded and won black studies. Poets, playwrights, musicians, painters and other artists created a new black aesthetics and ardently proclaimed that "black is beautiful."

No area of the African-American community escaped Malcolm's influence. The mainstream black leaders who dismissed him as a rabble-rouser today embrace his cultural philosophy and urge blacks to love themselves first before they even think about loving others. No one loved blacks more than Malcolm nor taught us more about ourselves. Before Malcolm most blacks wanted nothing to do with Africa. But he taught us that "you can't hate the roots of the tree and not hate the tree; you can't hate your origin and not end up hating yourself; you can't hate Africa and not hate yourself." A simple, profound truth; one that blacks needed (and still need) to hear. And no one said it as effectively as Malcolm X.

Early Life

Who was Malcolm X? He was born Malcolm Little in Omaha, Nebraska, on May 19, 1925. His father, J. Early

Little, was a Baptist preacher and a dedicated organizer for Marcus Garvey's Universal Negro Improvement Association. His mother, M. Louise Norton, also a Garveyite, was a West Indian from Grenada.

The Little family was driven out of Omaha by the Ku Klux Klan before Malcolm reached his first birthday. Another white hate group, called the Black Legion, burned down the Little's house in Lansing, Michigan, during Malcolm's childhood. Malcolm described the experience as "the nightmare in 1929." Soon after, his father was killed, thrown under a street car by the Black Legionnaires, Malcolm reported in his Autobiography.

With no husband, without the proceeds of his life insurance policy (the company refused to pay) and faced with constant harassment by the state welfare officials, Louise Little, a very proud woman, broke down under the emotional and economic strain of caring for eight children during the Depression. The Little children became wards of the state. Six of them, including Malcolm, were placed in foster homes. Malcolm's delinquent behavior eventually landed him in a detention home in Mason, Michigan, where he was allowed to attend junior high. He was the only black in his class. Although Malcolm was an outstanding student and extremely popular among his peers, he dropped out of school when his white eighth grade English teacher discouraged him from becoming a lawyer and suggested carpentry as a more "realistic goal for a nigger."

From Michigan, Malcolm journeyed to Boston and then to New York where he became known as "Detroit Red." He was involved in a life of crime—numbers, dope, con games of many kinds and thievery of all sorts, including armed robbery. Malcolm described himself as "one of the most depraved parasitical hustlers" in New York—"nervy and cunning enough to live by my wits, exploiting any prey that presented itself." A few months before he reached his 21st birthday, Malcolm was convicted and sentenced to eight to ten years in a Massachusetts prison for burglary.

Black Pride

In prison Malcolm's life was transformed when he discovered (through the influence of an inmate) the liberating value of education and (through his family) the empowering message of Elijah Muhammad's Nation of Islam. Both gave him what he did not have: self-respect as a black person. For the first time since attending the Garvey meetings with his father, Malcolm was proud to be black and to learn about Africans who "built great empires and civilizations and cultures."

Discovering knowledge through reading raised Malcolm's consciousness. He found out that history had been "whitened" and blacks had been left out. "It's a crime," Malcolm said, expressing his anger, "the lie that has been told to generations of blacks and whites. Little innocent black children born of parents who believed that their race had no history. Little black children seeing, before they could talk, that their parents considered themselves inferior. Innocent little black children growing up, living out their lives, dying of old age—and all their lives ashamed of being black."

Malcolm pledged while in prison to use his intellectual resources to destroy black self-hate and to replace it with black self-esteem. He transformed his prison cell into a hall of learning where he educated himself about "the brainwashed condition of blacks" and the crimes which "the devil white man" had committed against them. He was so engrossed in his studies that he even forgot he was in prison. "In every free moment I had," Malcolm reflected, "if I was not reading in the library, I was reading on my bunk. You couldn't have gotten me out of books with a wedge."

It was also in prison that Malcolm developed his debating skills. Debating, he said, was "like being on a battlefield—with intellectual and philosophical bullets." He became so effective in public speaking that even his opponents had to acknowledge his talent. Martin Luther King, Jr., and other mainstream civil rights leaders refused to appear on the same platform with him. People who did debate him

Malcolm X

often regretted it. For Malcolm there was no place for moderation or disinterested objectivity when one's freedom is at stake. "You can't negotiate upon freedom," he said. "You either fight for it or shut up."

The Nation of Islam

After his release from prison in 1952 Malcolm became a minister in the Nation of Islam and its most effective recruiter and apologist. In June 1954 Elijah Muhammad appointed Malcolm the head minister of the influential Temple Number 7 in Harlem. Speaking regularly in the Temple and at many street-corner rallies, Malcolm told Harlemites that "we are black first and everything else second." "We are not Americans," he said. "We are Africans who happen to be in America. We didn't land on Plymouth Rock. That rock landed on us."

Malcolm's primary audience was the "little black people in the street," the ones at the "bottom of the social heap." His message was harsh and bitter, a "sharp truth" that "cuts" and "causes great pain." "But if you can take the truth," he assured Harlem blacks, "it will cure you and save you from an otherwise certain death." Malcolm told them that they were "zombies, walking dead people," who had been cut off from any knowledge of their past history. "We have been robbed deaf, dumb and blind to the true knowledge of ourselves. We do not even know our names or our original language. We carry the slavemasters' names and speak their language. We even accepted the slavemasters' religion of Christianity, which teaches us that black is a curse. How can a people make others treat and respect them as human beings if they are culturally and spiritually dead?"

After describing their zombie-like state, Malcolm commanded blacks to "wake up" to "their humanity, to their own worth, and to their cultural heritage." He also told them to "clean up" themselves of drunkenness, profanity, drugs, crime and other moral failings. A resurrected, morally upright black people will be able to "stand up" and "do something for themselves instead of sitting around and waiting for white people to solve our problems and tell us we are free." Initially, Malcolm's black nationalist message was very unpopular in the African-American community. The media (both white and black) portrayed him as a teacher of hate and a promoter of violence. It was the age of integration, and love and nonviolence were advocated as the only way to achieve it. Most blacks shared Martin Luther King, Jr.'s dream that they would soon enter the mainstream of American society. They really believed that the majority of whites were genuinely sorry for what America had done to blacks and were now ready to right the wrongs and to treat blacks as human beings.

"The Religion of Naked, Undressed Truth"
Malcolm did not share the optimism of the civil rights movement and thus found himself speaking to many

unsympathetic audiences. He did not mind speaking against the dominant mood of the time as long as he knew that he was speaking the truth. He defined the Nation of Islam as "the religion of naked, undressed truth." "You shall know the truth and the truth shall make you free" was his favorite biblical passage. "If you are afraid to tell truth," he railed at his audience, "you don't deserve freedom." With truth on his side, Malcolm relished the odds that were against him. His task was to wake up "dead Negroes" by revealing to them the truth about America and about themselves.

The enormity of this challenge motivated Malcolm to attack head-on the philosophy of Martin King and the civil rights movement. He dismissed the charge that he was teaching hate: "It is the man who has made a slave out of you who is teaching hate." He rejected integration: "An integrated cup of coffee is insufficient pay for 400 years of slave labor." He denounced nonviolence as "the philosophy of a fool": "There is no philosophy more befitting to the white man's tactics for keeping his foot on the black man's neck." He ridiculed King's 1963 "I have a dream" speech: "While King was having a dream, the rest of us Negroes are having a nightmare." He also rejected as inhuman King's command to love the enemy: "It is not possible to love a man whose chief purpose in life is to humiliate you and still be considered a normal human being."

As long as Malcolm stayed in the Black Muslim movement he was not entirely free to speak his own mind. He had to represent Elijah Muhammad, the sole and absolute authority in the Nation of Islam. But in December 1963 Malcolm disobeyed Muhammad and described President Kennedy's assassination as an instance of the "Chickens coming home to roost." Muhammad rebuked him and used the incident as an opportunity to silence his star pupil—first for 90 days and then indefinitely. Malcolm soon realized that much more was involved in his silence than what he had said about the Kennedy assassination. Jealousy and envy in Muhammad's family circle were the primary motives behind his silencing, and this meant the ban would never be lifted.

For the sake of black people who needed to hear the message of black self-worth he was so adept in proclaiming, Malcolm reluctantly declared his independence in March 1964. His break with the Black Muslim movement was an important turning point. He was now free to develop his own philosophy of the black freedom struggle.

Black Revolution

Malcolm, however, had already begun to show independent thinking in his great "Message to the Grass Roots" speech, given in Detroit three weeks before his silencing. In that speech he endorsed black nationalism as his political philosophy, thereby separating himself not only from the civil rights movement but, more important, from Muhammad, who had defined the Nation as strictly religious and apolitical. Malcolm contrasted "the black revolution" with "the Negro revolution." The black revolution, he said, is "worldwide," and it is "bloody," "hostile" and "knows no compromise." But the so-called Negro revolution is not even a revolution. Malcolm mocked it: "The only revolution in which the goal is loving your enemy is the Negro revolution. It's the only revolution in which the goal is a desegregated lunch counter, a desegregated theater, a desegregated public park, a desegregated public toilet; you can sit down next to white folks on the toilet." He smiled as the audience broke into hearty laughter at this.

After his break with Muhammad, Malcolm developed more fully his cultural and political black nationalist philosophy in a speech titled, "The Ballot or the Bullet." In urging blacks to exercise their constitutional right to vote, he made a move toward King and the civil rights movement. Later he became more explicit: "Dr. King wants the same thing I want—freedom." Malcolm wanted to join the civil rights movement in order to expand it into a human rights movement, thereby internationalizing the black freedom struggle, making it more radical and more militant.

During his period of independence from the Nation of Islam nothing influenced Malcolm more than his travels abroad. He visited countries in the Middle East, Africa and Europe, where he explained the black struggle for justice in the U.S. and linked it with liberation struggles throughout the world. "You can't understand what is going on in Mississippi if you don't know what is going on in the Congo," he told Harlem blacks. "They are both the same. The same interests are at stake."

On February 21, 1965, Malcolm X was shot down by assassins as he started to speak to a crowd of 400 blacks at the Audubon Ballroom in Harlem. He was only 39.

Malcolm's Influence Today

Although dead for nearly 27 years, Malcolm's influence in the African-American community is much greater today than during his lifetime. His most far-reaching impact was among the masses of African-Americans in the ghettos of American cities. He told them, as James Baldwin observed, that "they should be proud of being black and God knows they should be. This is a very important thing to hear in a country that assures you that you should be ashamed of it." Saying what Malcolm meant to her, a Harlemite said: "He taught me that I was more than a Little Black Sambo or kinky hair or nigger."

There is a resurgence of interest in Malcolm in every segment of the African-American community, especially among those who were not yet born when he died. His name, words and face adorn T-shirts, buttons and the cover of rap records. His writings, books about him and tapes of his speeches are sold by street vendors, at cultural festivals and in bookstores. Wherever black people gather to talk about their struggle for justice, the ghost of Malcolm's presence is there, reminding us of the strengths and weaknesses of our past and present efforts. The more we reflect on the meaning of Malcolm's life and message the more we realize the greatness of his legacy.

Malcolm was a cultural revolutionary, an artist of the spoken word. Maya Angelou aptly called him "a charismatic speaker who could play an audience as great musicians play instruments." Peter Bailey said he was a "Master Teacher." Alfred Duckett called him "our sage and our saint." In his eulogy Ossie Davis bestowed upon Malcolm the title: "Our Shining Black Prince." For me, Malcolm was a cultural prophet of blackness. African-Americans who are proud to be black should thank Malcolm for creating the cultural space that lets us claim our African heritage.

All Americans owe Malcolm a great debt. He was not a racist, as many misguided observers have claimed. He was an uncompromising truth-teller whose love for his people empowered him to respect all human beings. "I am for truth," he said, "no matter who tells it. I am for justice no matter who is for or against it. I am a human being first and foremost, and as such I am for whoever and whatever benefits humanity as a whole."

An Independent Black Community

Malcolm X

In the early sixties, Malcolm X worked with journalist and novelist Alex Haley to produce *The Autobiography of Malcolm X*, published in 1964. The autobiography describes Malcolm's metamorphosis from an obscure, petty criminal to one of the most compelling—and implacable—voices for disfranchised blacks. Indeed, perhaps more than any other civil rights leader, Malcolm X articulated the intense frustration experienced by millions of blacks mired in poverty and second-class citizenship. The following excerpt from his autobiography summarizes Malcolm's approach to what he considered irreconcilable relations between the races: Charging that whites would never allow blacks to fully participate in the social and political fabric of society, he denounces integration as a remedy to black grievances. Only through separation and self-determination, rather, can blacks elevate themselves from subservience and build a self-respecting black community.

❦ ❦ ❦

T he Deep South white press generally blacked me out. But they front-paged what I felt about Northern white and black Freedom Riders going *South* to "demonstrate." I called it "ridiculous"; their own Northern ghettoes, right at home, had enough rats and roaches to kill to keep all of the Freedom Riders busy. I said that ultra-liberal New York had more integration problems than Mississippi. If the Northern Freedom Riders wanted more to do, they could work on the roots of such ghetto evils as the little children out in the streets at midnight, with apartment keys on strings around their necks to let themselves in, and their mothers and fathers drunk, drug addicts, thieves, prostitutes. Or the Northern Freedom Riders could light some fires under Northern city halls, unions, and major industries to give more jobs to Negroes to remove so many of them from the relief and welfare rolls, which created laziness, and which deteriorated the ghettoes into steadily worse places for humans to live. It was all—it *is* all—the absolute truth; but what did I want to *say* it for? Snakes couldn't have turned on me faster than the liberal.

Yes, I will pull off that liberal's halo that he spends such efforts cultivating! The North's liberals have been for so long pointing accusing fingers at the South and getting away with it that they have fits when they are exposed as the world's worst hypocrites.

I believe my own life *mirrors* this hypocrisy. I know nothing about the South. I am a creation of the Northern white man and of his hypocritical attitude toward the Negro.

The white Southerner was always given his due by Mr. Muhammad. The white Southerner, you can say one thing—he is honest. He bares his teeth to the black man; he tells the black man, to his face, that Southern whites never will accept phony "integration." The Southern white goes further, to tell the black man that he means to fight him every inch of the way—against even the so-called "tokenism." The advantage of this is the Southern black man never has been under any illusions about the opposition he is dealing with.

You can say for many Southern white people that, individually, they have been paternalistically helpful to many individual Negroes. But the Northern white man, he grins with his teeth, and his mouth has always been full of tricks and lies of "equality" and "integration." When one day all over America, a black hand touched the white man's shoulder, and the white man turned, and there stood the Negro saying "Me, too . . ." why, that Northern liberal shrank from that black man with as much guilt and dread as any Southern white man.

Northern Black Ghettoes

Actually, America's most dangerous and threatening black man is the one who has been kept sealed up by the Northerner in the black ghettoes—the Northern white power structure's system to keep talking democracy while keeping the black man out of sight somewhere, around the corner.

The word "integration" was invented by a Northern liberal. The word has no real meaning. I ask you: in the racial sense in which it's used so much today, whatever "integration" is supposed to mean, can it precisely be defined? The truth is that "integration" is an *image*, it's a foxy Northern liberal's smoke-screen that confuses the true wants of the American black man. Here in these fifty racist and neo-racist states of North America, this word "integration" has millions of white people confused, and angry, believing wrongly that the black masses want to live mixed up with the white man. That is the case only with the relative handful of these "integration"-mad Negroes.

I'm talking about these "token-integrated" Negroes who flee from their poor, downtrodden black brothers— from their own self-hate, which is what they're really trying to escape. I'm talking about these Negroes you will see who can't get enough of nuzzling up to the white man. These "chosen few" Negroes are more white-minded, more anti-black, than even the white man is.

Human rights! Respect as *human beings!* That's what America's black masses want. That's the true problem. The black masses want not to be shrunk from as though they are plague-ridden. They want not to be walled up in slums, in the ghettoes, like animals. They want to live in an open, free society where they can walk with their heads up, like men, and women!

Few white people realize that many black people to-day dislike and avoid spending any more time than they must around white people. This "integration" image, as it is popularly interpreted, has millions of vain, self-exalted white people convinced that black people want to sleep in bed with them—and that's a lie! Or you can't *tell* the average white man that the Negro man's prime desire isn't to have a white woman—another lie! . . .

The black masses prefer the company of their own kind. Why, even these fancy, bourgeois Negroes—when they get back home from the fancy "integrated" cocktail parties, what do they do but kick off their shoes and talk about those white liberals they just left as if the liberals were dogs. And the white liberals probably do the very same thing. I can't be sure about the whites, I am never around them in private—but the bourgeois Negroes know I'm not lying.

I'm telling it like it *is!* You *never* have to worry about me biting my tongue if something I know as truth is on my mind. Raw, naked truth exchanged between the black man and the white man is what a whole lot more of is needed in this country—to clear the air of the racial mirages, clichés, and lies that this country's very atmosphere has been filled with for four hundred years.

In many communities, especially small communities,

white people have created a benevolent image of themselves as having had so much "good-will toward our
Negroes," every time any "local Negro" begins suddenly letting the local whites know the truth—that the
black people are sick of being hind-tit, second-class,
disfranchised, that's when you hear, uttered so sadly,
"Unfortunately now because of this, our whites of
good-will are starting to turn against the Negroes. . . .
It's so regrettable . . . progress *was* being made . . . but
now our communications between the races have broken down!"

Communication Between the Races

What are they talking about? There never was any *communication*. Until after World War II, there wasn't a
single community in the entire United States where the
white man heard from any local Negro "leaders" the
truth of what Negroes felt about the conditions that the
white community imposed upon Negroes.

You need some proof? Well, then, why was it that
when Negroes did start revolting across America, virtually all of white America was caught up in surprise and
even shock? I would hate to be general of an army as
badly informed as the American white man has been
about the Negro in this country.

This is the situation which permitted Negro combus-
tion to slowly build up to the revolution-point, without
the white man realizing it. All over America, the local
Negro "leader," in order to survive as a "leader," kept
reassuring the local white man, in effect, "Everything's
all right, everything's right in hand, boss!" When the
"leader" wanted a little something for his people: "Er,
boss, some of the people talking about we sure need a
better school, boss." And if the local Negroes hadn't
been causing any "trouble," the "benevolent" white man
might nod and give them a school, or some jobs.

The white men belonging to the power structures in thousands of communities across America know that I'm right! They know that I am describing what has been the true pattern of "communications" between the "local whites of good-will" and the local Negroes. It has been a pattern created by domineering, ego-ridden whites. Its characteristic design permitted the white man to feel "noble" about throwing crumbs to the black man, instead of feeling guilty about the local community's system of cruelly exploiting Negroes.

But I want to tell you something. This pattern, this "system" that the white man created, of teaching Negroes to hide the truth from him behind a façade of grinning, "yessir-bossing," foot-shuffling and head-scratching— that system has done the American white man more harm than an invading army would do to him.

Why do I say this? Because all this has steadily helped this American white man to build up, deep in his psyche, absolute conviction that he *is* "superior." In how many, many communities have, thus, white men who didn't finish high school regarded condescendingly university-educated local Negro "leaders," principals of schools, teachers, doctors, other professionals?

The white man's system has been imposed upon non-white peoples all over the world. This is exactly the reason why wherever people who are anything but white live in this world today, the white man's governments are finding themselves in deeper and deeper trouble and peril.

Let's just face truth. Facts! Whether or not the white man of the world is able to face truth, and facts, about the true reasons for his troubles—that's what essentially will determine whether or not *he* will now survive.

Today we are seeing this revolution of the non-white peoples, who just a few years ago would have frozen in horror if the mighty white nations so much as lifted an eyebrow. What it is, simply, is that black and brown and red and yellow peoples have, after hundreds of years of exploitation and imposed "inferiority" and general misuse, become, finally, do-or-die sick and tired of the white man's heel on their necks.

How can the white American government figure on selling "democracy" and "brotherhood" to non-white peoples—if they read and hear every day what's going on right here in America, and see the better-than-a-thousand-words photographs of the American white man denying "democracy" and "brotherhood" even to America's native-born non-whites? The world's non-whites know how this Negro here has loved the American white man, and slaved for him, tended to him, nursed him. This Negro has jumped into uniform and gone off and died when this America was attacked by enemies both white and non-white. Such a faithful, loyal non-white as *this*—and *still* America bombs him, and sets dogs on him, and turns fire hoses on him, and jails him by the thousands, and beats him bloody, and inflicts upon him all manner of other crimes.

Of course these things, known and refreshed every day for the rest of the world's non-whites, are a vital factor in these burnings of ambassadors' limousines, these stonings, defilings, and wreckings of embassies and legations, these shouts of "White man, go home!" these attacks on white Christian missionaries, and these bombings and tearing down of flags.

Is it clear why I have said that the American white man's malignant superiority complex has done him more harm than an invading army?

Black Independence

The American black man should be focusing his every effort toward building his *own* businesses, and decent homes for himself. As other ethnic groups have done, let the black people, wherever possible, however possible, patronize their own kind, hire their own kind, and start in those ways to build up the black race's ability to do for itself. That's the only way the American black man is ever going to get respect. One thing the white man never can give the black man is self-respect! The black man never can become independent and recognized as a human being who is truly equal with other human beings until he has what they have, and until he is doing for himself what others are doing for themselves.

The black man in the ghettoes, for instance, has to start self-correcting his own material, moral, and spiritual defects and evils. The black man needs to start his own program to get rid of drunkenness, drug addiction, prostitution. The black man in America has to lift up his own sense of values.

Only a few thousands of Negroes, relatively a very tiny number, are taking any part in "integration." Here, again, it is those few bourgeois Negroes, rushing to throw away their little money in the white man's luxury hotels, his swanky nightclubs, and big, fine, exclusive restaurants. The white people patronizing those places can afford it. But these Negroes you see in those places can't afford it, certainly most of them can't. Why, what does some Negro one installment payment away from disaster look like somewhere downtown out to dine, grinning at some headwaiter who has more money than the Negro? Those bourgeois Negroes out draping big tablecloth-sized napkins over their knees and ordering quail under glass and stewed snails—why, Negroes don't even *like* snails! What they're doing is proving they're integrated.

The Ballot or the Bullet

Malcolm X

With his commanding presence and emphatic use of words, Malcolm X was a popular public speaker. On March 29, 1964, Easter Sunday, a large audience turned out to hear Malcolm speak in the Audubon Ballroom in New York. The address was short but terse. Calling for equal opportunity and warning that "It's going to be the ballot or the bullet," Malcolm's words were picked up by the press and the phrase became the slogan of black militant groups across the country. Less than a year later, Malcolm's life was cut short by an assassin's bullet as he spoke in the same ballroom from which he delivered the now famous "ballot or the bullet" speech.

🐾 🐾 🐾

It is very very heartening and encouraging for me to see so many of our people take time to come out, especially on Easter Sunday night. You and I are not a people who are used to going anywhere on Easter night—or on Easter Sunday night—to hear anything to do with African-Americans, or so-called Negroes.

One of the reasons that it is bad for us to continue to just refer to ourselves as the so-called Negro, that's negative. When we say so-called Negro that's pointing out what we aren't, but it isn't telling us what we are. We are Africans, and we happen to be in America. We are not Americans. We are a people who formerly were Africans who were kidnaped and brought to America. Our forefathers weren't the Pilgrims. We didn't land on Plymouth Rock; the rock was landed on us. We were brought here against our will; we were not brought here to be made citizens. We were not brought here to enjoy the constitutional gifts that they speak so beautifully about today. Because we weren't brought here to be made citizens—today, now that we've become awakened to some degree, and we begin to ask for those things which they say are supposedly for all Americans, they look upon us with a hostility and unfriendliness.

So our unwanted presence—the fact that we are unwanted is becoming magnified in all of America's preachments today and the only way that we who are . . . [interruption]

The first step for those of us who believe in the philosophy of Black Nationalism is to realize that the problem begins right here. The first problem is right here. We have to elevate our thinking right here first— not just the thinking of a handful, that won't do it. But the thinking of 22 million black people in this country must be elevated. They must be made to see it as we see it. They must be made to think as we think, and then they'll be ready to act just as we're ready to act.

The black nationalists don't realize this. The black nationalists will fail as other groups have failed. Any philosophy that you have that can't be implemented is no good. A "preaching" or a gospel is no better than its ability to be carried out in a manner that will make it beneficial to the people who accept it.

When you have a philosophy or a gospel—I don't care whether it's a religious gospel, a political gospel, an economic gospel or a social gospel—if it's not going to do something for you and me right here and right now—to hell with that gospel! In the past, most of the religious gospels that you and I have heard have benefitted only those who preach it. Most of the political gospels that you and I have heard have benefitted only the politicians. The social gospels have benefitted only the sociologists.

You and I need something right now that's going to benefit all of us. That's going to change the community in which we live, not try to take us somewhere else. If we can't live here, we never will live somewhere else.

Nationalism
Number one: Why is it so difficult to get so many of our people in this country interested in going to Africa? And I have to point this out because today the entire question has reached a new level of thought. There was a time when you talked about going to Africa, and you heard about it out on the corner—125th Street and 7th Avenue. But today on college campuses across the country you have students who are interested in nationalism. Nationalism is the wave of the present and the future. It is nationalism that is bringing freedom to oppressed people all over the world. It was nationalism that brought freedom to the Algerians. It was nationalism that brought freedom to the Nigerians and to the Ghanaians. It was nationalism that brought freedom to the people of Uganda and Tanganyika and Sudan and Somaliland. It was nationalism that has brought about the freedom of every oppressed people. They have studied the tactics and the strategy and the message of all of the African nations who have emerged and have won their independence. And they have seen that the

Africans did not get it by sitting in. They did not get it by waiting in. They did not get it by singing, "We Shall Overcome"; they got it through nationalism. And you and I will get it through nationalism.

What is it that makes it difficult for the philosophy of nationalism to spread among the so-called Negroes? Number one, they think they have a stake in America. They think they have an investment in this country. Which we do: We've invested 310 years of slave labor. 310 years, every day of which your and my mother and father worked for nothing. Not eight hours a day—there was no union in that day. They worked from sunup until sundown—from can't see in the morning until can't see at night. They never had a day off! And on Sunday they were allowed to sit down and sing about when they died they wouldn't be slaves no more—when they died, they wouldn't be slaves no more. They'd go up in the sky and every day would be Sunday. That's a shame.

And it is that 310 years of slave labor that was my and your contribution into this particular economy and political system.

You and I should let them know now that either we collect our investment right here, right now, and then if we can't collect it here, our people will then be ready to go back home. Let's go ahead and join in with them and make these men pay these back wages. Make him give us the back pay.

Let's join in—if this is what the Negro wants, let's join him. Let's show him how to struggle. Let's show him how to fight. Let's show him how to bring a real revolution.

Let's make him stop jiving!

A Call to Action

If you're interested in freedom, you need some judo, you need some karate—you need all the things that will help you fight for freedom. If we don't resort to the bullet, then immediately we have to take steps to use the ballot. Equality of opportunity, if the constitution at the present time [doesn't offer it], then change it. Either it offers it, or it doesn't offer it. If it offers it—good, then give it to us—if it doesn't offer it, then change it. You don't need a debate. You don't need a filibuster. You need some action!

So what you and I have to do is get involved. You and I have to be right there breathing down their throats. Every time they look over their shoulders, we want them to see us.

We want to make them—we want to make them—pass the strongest civil-rights bill they ever passed, because we know that even after they pass it, they can't enforce it.

In order to do this, we're starting a voters' registration drive. We have to get everybody in Harlem registered, not as Democrats or Republicans, but registered as Independents. We're going to organize a corps of brothers and sisters who, after this city is mapped out, they won't leave one apartment-house door not knocked on. There won't be a door in Harlem that will not have been knocked on to see that whatever black face lives behind that door is registered to vote by a certain time this year. Nobody will have an excuse not to be registered. We'll ask him to let us see your card. If you don't have the sense of responsibility to get registered, we'll move you out of town.

It's going to be the ballot or the bullet.

CHAPTER

4

Profiles · in · History

Other Leaders

Thurgood Marshall: Legal Strategist

James J. Flynn

In the 1930s, as the National Association for the Advancement of Colored People (NAACP) was gathering momentum to dismantle the legal foundations that supported segregation and discrimination, a brilliant young attorney came to the fore: Thurgood Marshall, recently graduated from the prestigious Howard Law School, joined the staff of the NAACP in 1935. As chief counsel of the civil rights organization from 1940 to 1961, Marshall used a variety of legal strategies in a drive to end segregation in housing, employment, voting, and education. He won several crucial cases, most notably the historic *Brown v. Board of Education*, which rendered segregation in public schools illegal. Marshall later became the first African American justice to sit on the Supreme Court of the United States. James J. Flynn is the author of *Negroes of Achievement in Modern America*. In the following profile, Flynn highlights Marshall's stellar career with the NAACP—and how he used the courts to promote social equality.

❧   ❧   ❧

In 1935, [Thurgood] Marshall was invited to join the legal staff of the National Association for the Advancement of Colored People [NAACP]. It was an exciting offer, because Dean Houston [of Howard University, where Marshall had attended law school] had resigned from Howard to assume the position of chief counsel for the NAACP. When Thurgood Marshall decided to accept the offer, little did he ever dream where the assignment would lead him and what he would be able to accomplish for the civil rights movement. Those early days with the NAACP were not filled with great prospects. It was going to be a long, hard road to follow unswervingly.

Marshall's first important victory came in 1936, in the case of *Pearson v. Murray*. Donald Murray, a Negro, had applied for enrollment in the University of Maryland Law School and was rejected. For Thurgood, this was a work that came close to his heart—he remembered his own rejection by the [University of] Maryland Law School. Marshall sought the help of Dean Houston in preparing his case. It was a well-briefed case. The proof of this was the decision of the Maryland Court of Appeals, which held that the state must afford equal educational opportunities in its institutions.

The Power of the Courts

It has always been the sincere belief of Thurgood Marshall that it will be through the courts that the black man will achieve rightful equality. To this young constitutional lawyer, the Fourteenth Amendment was added to the Constitution to give the black man his full rights as an American citizen. He felt it was his duty as a lawyer to make the Supreme Court reflect the real America in civil rights cases covered by the "equal protection" clause of the Fourteenth Amendment.

Thurgood Marshall risked his life many times in the

first few years of his tenure with the NAACP. He is not unwilling to admit that he was afraid during some of his experiences. After he was threatened in this way in relation to a case he was trying in Shreveport, Louisiana, he commented, "I wrapped my constitutional rights in cellophane, tucked them in my hip pocket and got out of sight. And, believe me, I caught the next train out of town." This was only a temporary setback, for, inevitably, he was around to fight again another day.

The power that kept Marshall going during this trying period was his infinite capacity for hard work. His tremendous sense of humor was a great asset, too, in helping him to keep his equilibrium. He traveled 50,000 miles a year, being away from his office most of the time. The hours he spent before the Supreme Court were filled with tension and pressure. When his court appearances were over, he became the happy, effervescent type that he had been back at Lincoln University.

All the efforts of Thurgood Marshall during his first seven years with the NAACP were not devoted to civil rights cases. Labor matters took a good percentage of his time. He won a suit against a union which used closed-shop contracts to discriminate against Negroes. He also moved into the question of discrimination in the Air Corps. His victory in this case eventually led to complete desegregation in the armed forces. It was Thurgood Marshall who fought the Democratic party of Texas until it opened its former all-white primaries to blacks.

Desegregating Education

Their interest in various areas of civil rights kept bringing the thinking Negroes back to the area of desegregation in education. Marshall and his colleagues in the NAACP decided to begin the campaign at the graduate level of education. The reason behind this was a sound

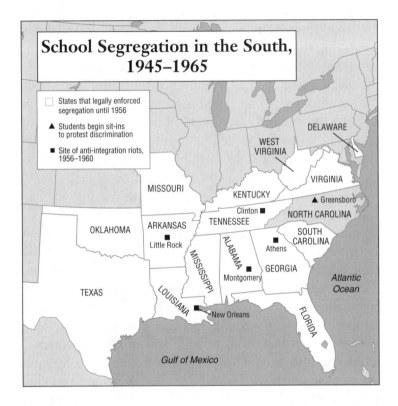

School Segregation in the South, 1945–1965

☐ States that legally enforced segregation until 1956

▲ Students begin sit-ins to protest discrimination

■ Site of anti-integration riots, 1956–1960

DELAWARE

WEST VIRGINIA

VIRGINIA

MISSOURI

KENTUCKY

▲ Greensboro

Clinton ■

NORTH CAROLINA

TENNESSEE

OKLAHOMA

ARKANSAS

SOUTH CAROLINA

Little Rock ■

MISSISSIPPI

ALABAMA

Athens ■

GEORGIA

Montgomery ■

TEXAS

LOUISIANA

■ New Orleans

FLORIDA

Atlantic Ocean

Gulf of Mexico

one. There were fewer students involved here, so the opposition would be proportionately less. As usual, it proved to be a slow process. First, the leaders had to get someone who was willing to bring the suit, then they had to move it all the way through the lower courts until it reached the Supreme Court.

The plaintiff was found when a young man named Herman Swealt agreed to bring a suit against Texas segregation. The case was known as *Swealt v. Painter*, and in 1950 the Supreme Court ordered the plaintiff admitted to the University of Texas Law School. The decision stated that the all-black law school of Texas State University for Negroes was inferior to the all-white University of Texas Law School in such areas as community standing, tradition, and prestige. On the same day, in a case titled *McLaurin v. Oklahoma State Regents*, the Supreme Court called for the same treatment of black students as was given to those of other races in the University of Oklahoma Graduate School. G.W. McLaurin was in the school, but he had been forced to attend segregated classes.

The year 1951 was a busy one for Thurgood Marshall. He spent many weeks in Korea, checking charges that men from a black regiment were being discriminated against. In fact, several had been court-martialed, and one of them had been sentenced to death. Marshall worked on these cases and sought evidence right up to the front lines. He was able to get acquittals or reduced sentences for over half of the convicted.

Arriving back in the United States, Marshall gave his entire efforts to the school desegregation problem. Realizing that the Supreme Court was moving they knew not where, the southern leaders hurried to make their school systems meet the requirements of *Plessy v. Ferguson*. Back in 1896, the Supreme Court had declared in *Plessy v. Ferguson*, that as long as the accommodations for whites and blacks were equal, they could be separate. This was the theory that Thurgood Marshall was fighting to overcome.

He felt that the sure way to kill *Plessy v. Ferguson* was to show that desegregation in education was indeed unequal. This could only be done by presenting a mountain of evidence from professionals. Marshall and his assistants gathered their evidence from sociologists, psychologists, psychiatrists, and anthropologists. Their general consensus was that the equal but separate concept played havoc with the feelings of members of the black race. The reports of these professionals formed the basis for the cases eventually presented by Marshall to the Supreme Court.

These cases all arose out of separate attacks on *Plessy*

v. Ferguson in Kansas, South Carolina, Virginia, and Delaware. The Supreme Court took these four school appeals and heard the first argument during the October, 1962, session.

Brown v. Board of Education

The lead-off case, which bore the name of the four suits, was known as *Brown v. Board of Education of Topeka.* Oliver Brown was the father of an eight-year-old girl who was not permitted to attend an all-white school five blocks from her home. Instead, she had to travel twenty-one blocks away, to an all-black school. Her parents were asking that this segregation be stopped. The United States District Court for Kansas refused on the "separate but equal" ruling contained in *Plessy v. Ferguson.* The other three state decisions were about the same. This left the door open for appeals to the Supreme Court.

Final arguments were heard in December, 1953. Before Thurgood Marshall walked into the Supreme Court chamber to present his case, hundreds of hours had been spent by him and by his associates in carefully gathering and sifting the facts. Lawyer Marshall realized that one small slip, the misplacing of the right word in a single instance, could wreck the case. He presented a masterful brief in which he concluded that the only reason why the South wanted to keep segregation was the "inherent determination that the people who were formerly in slavery, regardless of anything else, shall be kept as near that stage as possible."

The other side of the issue was presented by John W. Davis, an eighty-year-old constitutional lawyer who had unsuccessfully run for president in 1924. His only argument was that the school question was not a federal problem, since it was purely a state function.

It was five months before the Supreme Court spoke. On May 17, 1954, a Monday, the Court was preparing to hand down one of its last decisions of the year. Reporters were told it would be a quiet day. Then, Chief Justice Earl Warren dropped a news bomb when he announced the unanimous decision on school desegregation. He explained how the court had been persuaded by the professional testimony that the separation of the races "generates a feeling of inferiority that may affect their hearts and minds in a way unlikely ever to be undone."

These were happy times for Thurgood Marshall. He was now seeing the results of the months and months of careful, tedious planning paying off. Those lectures of Dean Houston that called for hard work and sound logic had won the day. The Supreme Court had given the southern states until October 1, 1954, to indicate how they were going to carry out the order. The NAACP was also to file its thoughts on the subject.

Personal Tragedy

Between the time the order of the Court was filed and the pronouncement in the spring of 1955, tragedy struck the Marshall family. Thurgood had noticed that his wife Buster was gradually losing weight and was always complaining of being tired. The family physician informed him that his wife had terminal lung cancer. In order to spare him the shock of this sad news while he was preparing and presenting the school case, Buster would not permit the doctor to tell Thurgood until after the Supreme Court reached a decision. In the weeks that preceded her death in February, 1955, Marshall was in a state of shock. Afterwards, he remained in seclusion, refusing to leave his apartment in Harlem for weeks on end, and reliving the twenty-six years of happy married life he had shared with his wife.

Marshall's personal sorrow had added to it the realization that the southern states were in no hurry to carry out the Supreme Court's directions. This was brought home with a vengeance when Governor Orval Faubus, of Arkansas, refused to permit black students to enter all-white Center High School in Little Rock—this in spite of the Brown decision. It was only when President Eisenhower sent in Federal troops that the violence generated by segregationists was quelled.

Marshall was moved to action when the United States Court of Appeals, Eighth Circuit, issued an order to keep schools segregated for the time being. He appeared before Supreme Court Justice Charles E. Whittaker, demanding that the Court of Appeals order be revoked. He said it was about time that the Supreme Court be obeyed. Governor Faubus got the state legislature to pass a law authorizing the closing of the schools of Arkansas if the Supreme Court acted. While the nation marked time, President Eisenhower told a press conference that there should be "slower" movement toward integration in the schools. The NAACP members could not believe what they heard. Roy Wilkins, the executive secretary, could only consider the President's statement "incredible."

Following the Arkansas school decision, Marshall continued to work hard. It helped him to forget his sorrow at the loss of Buster. He continued to travel as much as 50,000 miles a year, and had his hand in as many as five or six hundred cases involving his race. Some thirty-two times he appeared to argue civil rights cases before the United States Supreme Court. In nine out of ten times, he came out the victor. He was the toast of the black community, where he was known as "Mr. Civil Rights." He was offered many lucrative private legal opportunities, but he preferred to stay with the NAACP.

On the Bench
The election of President John F. Kennedy made the offer of a federal judgeship to Thurgood Marshall al-

most a sure thing. This sort of an appointment had been suggested once before, in 1949, when the press declared that Thurgood Marshall's name was being considered for a federal judgeship. At that time, Marshall had refused to join a Democratic club in New York City, because it was suggested that this was necessary to get the appointment.

This same offer, now a firm one, was still looked upon with disdain by Marshall in 1961. In addition, he believed that if he went to the bench, he would be charged with deserting the civil rights cause. Eventually, however, he agreed to have his name presented to the Senate for confirmation. President Kennedy sent his name in on September 23, 1961, and the southerners on the Judiciary Committee announced they would not touch it until they returned from their recess, in January, 1962. To get around this deliberate delay, President Kennedy gave Marshall an interim appointment. This meant that while Congress was out of session, the President placed him on the bench. On October 24, 1961, hundreds of Thurgood Marshall's friends were present when he took the oath as a federal judge. Among those who watched with pride was Thurgood Marshall's second wife, Cecile Suyat Marshall. Cecile had been a secretary in the New York office of the NAACP. With her on this happy day were their two children, Thurgood, Jr., five, and John, three.

Congress returned in January, 1962, and the President sent to the Senate a strong endorsement of Thurgood Marshall as a federal judge, and the American Bar Association declared that he was "well qualified." In spite of all this, the Senate Judiciary Committee, led by Senator James O. Eastland, a Mississippi Democrat, did everything possible to stall the appointment. It was only after the New York Republican, Senator Kenneth B. Keating, declared, "A distinguished American jurist is being victimized," that in July, 1962, hearings on the nomination were scheduled.

Long and delaying tactics eventually forced the committee to report favorably on the appointment. When the Senate finally voted, on September 12, 1962, it was to seat Thurgood Marshall as a United States Court of Appeals Justice. It had taken almost one year to place this fighter for civil rights on the bench.

Four long years—and more than one hundred opinions—later, Thurgood Marshall was well established as a jurist. He found the bench much more restricting than his work with the NAACP. He missed the excitement of preparing and trying cases.

When President Lyndon B. Johnson telephoned Thurgood Marshall on July 7, 1965, and asked him to become Solicitor General of the United States, he accepted with alacrity and dispatch. In this position he was forced to take a cut of $4,500 in salary, but to compensate for this, he would be back before the Supreme Court, trying cases for the Government. He answered his friends who wondered why he left a lifetime job for one that could be lost with a change of administration: "The President asks you to go, you go." There was some negative southern reaction to the appointment, but not of the type that had been used to hold up his judicial appointment.

While he was Solicitor General, Thurgood Marshall performed for the Government as well as he had for the NAACP. His record shows that he won fourteen of the nineteen cases he presented to the Supreme Court. As the Government's chief appellate lawyer, when he appeared before the Court, he was listened to with attention by the justices.

It was on July 13, 1967, that President Johnson told a press conference that he intended to send the name of Thurgood Marshall to the Senate as the replacement for retiring Justice Tom C. Clark of the Supreme Court. President Johnson said of Marshall, "I believe he has already earned his place in history. But I think it will be greatly enhanced by his service on the Court . . . it is the right thing to do, the right time to do it, the right man, and the right place."

The story of prejudice was the same as before in the Senate. The southern bloc held five long hearings to decide whether Thurgood Marshall was fit to serve on the Court. On August 3, 1967, the Senate Judiciary Committee voted eleven to five to confirm the nomination. Four weeks later, the full Senate voted their approval sixty-nine to eleven. Upon receiving the news, Judge Marshall commented, "Let me take this opportunity to reaffirm my deep faith in this nation and its people, and to pledge that I shall ever be mindful of my obligation to the Constitution and to the goal of equal justice under law."

To fully understand and appreciate Thurgood Marshall's fight for civil rights, it must be remembered that it never included violence. Civil disobedience was never his way of accomplishing things. His deference for the law appproached the intensity of a dedicated man. It made it impossible for him to join the civil rights demonstrators. He achieved the goal in his own fine way.

Whitney Young Jr. and the Urban League

Dennis C. Dickerson

Whitney Young Jr. made huge strides in 1960s race relations. Reputed for his quiet diplomacy and persuasive speaking skills, Young was named executive director of the National Urban League in 1961, a position he held until his death in 1971. The league was founded in 1910 to expand career opportunities for African Americans. As its head, Young sought to reconcile the concerns of black America to white business and political leaders, stressing that black economic advancement would enhance the American experience not only for African Americans, but also for society as a whole. To this end, Young appealed to corporate America to support job programs, increased educational opportunities, and affordable housing for minorities. The following overview of Young's life—and critical role in the civil rights movement—is excerpted from Dennis C. Dickerson's book *Militant Mediator: Whitney M. Young Jr.*

❧ ❧ ❧

Black Americans seldom have spoken with a single voice. While a consensus has always existed concerning the urgency of freedom and equality, blacks have disagreed about how these objectives were to be achieved. During the black struggles of the 1950s and 1960s, despite intergroup conflicts, leaders of the major civil rights organizations spoke with rare unanimity about their quest for an integrated American society. Although they pursued common goals, they chose different tactics to attain them. Moreover, each played a special leadership role and made unique contributions to the civil rights movement.

These national leaders, the "Big Six," defined the goals of the civil rights struggle and encouraged blacks and whites to respond to the call for "Freedom Now." James Farmer of the Congress of Racial Equality (CORE), Martin Luther King Jr. of the Southern Christian Leadership Conference (SCLC), and John Lewis and James Forman, spokesmen for the Student Nonviolent Coordinating Committee (SNCC), represented activist organizations that used marches, freedom rides, sit-ins, and aggressive voter registration as their principal tactics. They believed that confrontations with racist institutions and protests against odious racial practices, particularly in the South, would result in progress for blacks. Although not on the frontline of civil rights protest, Dorothy Height headed an important federation of black women's groups, the National Council of Negro Women. She lent valuable support to efforts to achieve racial equality. Roy Wilkins served as the executive director of the oldest and largest civil rights group, the National Association for the Advancement of Colored People. Although the NAACP often sponsored marches, the organization stressed change through the legal and political system, particularly in the courts and through legislative lobbying.

Whitney M. Young Jr., the militant but diplomatic head of the National Urban League, also belonged to this leadership cadre. Like Farmer, King, and Forman, Young possessed impeccable activist credentials. In the early 1950s, while he served as executive director of the Omaha Urban League, he planned strategy with the combative De Porres Club, a forerunner of the Nebraska affiliate of CORE. Later in the decade, when he was dean of the School of Social Work at Atlanta University, he became an officer in the local NAACP and an adviser to student protesters who challenged racial segregation in downtown Atlanta stores. Young appreciated the importance of activism to achieve civil rights, and he supported these efforts throughout his career. At the same time, he asserted with equal fervor that the National Urban League with its programs for job training and social services was best equipped to translate de jure victories into de facto equality for black Americans.

A Different Type of Leader

Young's style of leadership differed significantly from that of King, Farmer, Wilkins, and Lewis and Forman. Other black leaders articulated the demands of black Americans with urgency and eloquence. Young voiced these same grievances, but he tried to reconcile them to the social and economic concerns of major white institutions. He interpreted the goals and grievances of black Americans to government, business, and foundations. He also sought ways to persuade powerful whites within these institutions that their support of the civil rights movement was consistent with their interests. He stressed that the achievement of political and economic equality would give blacks a stake in American society and would create a black middle class of entrepreneurs and consumers and a group of professional,

technical, and blue-collar workers whose skills and pro-
ductivity would enhance the American economy. While
he helped government, business, and foundation leaders understand black demands, he developed specific
programs to involve these officials in efforts to allay
racial tensions and to ameliorate the black social and
economic condition. Young was a black ambassador to
elite white leaders and institutions. He interpreted the
grievances and concerns of each group to the other. . . .

Major Influences

Three influences shaped the leadership of Whitney M.
Young Jr. First, his parents had a profound impact on
him. Loved and encouraged by both, he became a con-
fident adult unashamed of his race and unintimidated
by whites. From his father he learned how to negotiate
with influential whites and reconcile his objectives with
their interests. The elder Young headed Lincoln Institute in Lincoln Ridge, Kentucky. This secondary
school provided high school training to blacks from numerous Kentucky communities with limited educational facilities for their minority students. The elder
Young consciously emulated the pragmatism of Booker
T. Washington and his stress upon practical education.
Also, like the Tuskegeean, Young successfully courted
wealthy Kentucky whites and state officials and drew
needed support to his financially vulnerable institution.
By observing his father, Young learned how to negotiate skillfully and effectively with powerful whites. From
his mother, he learned that in some instances militant
confrontation with racial injustices was necessary.
Whenever her children were slighted or when a white
sales clerk treated her family discourteously, Laura Ray
Young almost never held her tongue. She also defended
Lincoln Institute students in their encounters with local police. She and her husband helped to mold Young

into a black leader skilled in the art of persuasion but ready to protest when white leaders and institutions seemed deaf to black demands.

The Urban League was the second major influence that shaped Young's leadership. He spent nearly two decades as an official in this organization. Established in 1911, the National Urban League grew rapidly in the 1920s and succeeding decades because it provided a wide range of employment and social services to recent black arrivals to the cities. Since individual philanthropists, foundations, and corporations traditionally financed the group, most League officials knew that effective dealings with wealthy whites were required for success. Additionally, negotiations with employers, unions, and various government units, especially about jobs for blacks, required diplomacy. Although Whitney Young injected greater militancy into the National Urban League and involved it in more controversial issues, he expanded corporate, foundation, and government contributions to the organization. His skill in presenting urgent racial issues in a nonconfrontational manner won him numerous supporters within these important institutions.

Escalating black militancy during the 1950s and 1960s was the third major influence on Young. The Brown decision of 1954, in which the Supreme Court outlawed public school segregation, inspired blacks to undertake greater activism to bring about the total demise of Jim Crow. One historian has written that the Brown decision was a "second emancipation proclamation" and that it "heightened the aspirations and expectations of Afro-Americans as nothing ever had before." A burgeoning civil rights movement resulted. The Baton Rouge, Montgomery, and Tallahassee bus boycotts of the 1950s, the Little Rock crisis of 1957, and the Greensboro sit-ins of 1960 mobilized blacks and sympathetic whites to demonstrate and protest until the federal government moved to end second-class citizenship for the nation's largest racial minority. When Young became executive director of the National Urban League in 1961, he wanted to revive a conservative organization that viewed its role as narrowly oriented toward social service. His desire to make this change came mainly from two sources. First, Young had experience as an activist. Second, the growing militancy of that civil rights struggle compelled him to make forthright statements in support of black demands for political and economic equality. With freedom rides, sit-ins, and marches occurring throughout the South and some parts of the North, Young wanted the National Urban League to get involved directly in the black struggle. He wanted blacks unmistakably to identify him and the National Urban League with such activist groups as CORE, SCLC, SNCC, and the NAACP. At the same time, Young was able to persuade powerful whites that in the midst of these unsettled racial conditions, the National Urban League was the best equipped organization to implement programs to achieve actual black equality. As a result, funds flowing into the civil rights movement went not only to such activist leaders as King, Farmer, and Forman and the groups they represented, but also to Whitney M. Young Jr. and the National Urban League.

Empowering Blacks

Young made a major contribution to the civil rights movement through his audacious advocacy of creative programs for racial advancement and as a gifted and effective organizer and mediator. He suggested in 1963, for example, that the federal government undertake a bold initiative, a "domestic Marshall Plan," and spend $145 million over the following decade to rehabilitate black Americans. In 1968 he secured from the Ford

Foundation a grant of $1,050,000 for the National Urban League to initiate a grassroots program relevant to the immediate needs of particular black communities. This "New Thrust" effort allowed the National Urban League "to change . . . from . . . a bridge between black and white communities to that of an advocate for . . . large, low-income ghetto areas." The League was to become less concerned with interpreting black demands to powerful whites than with developing the capacity of blacks to define their own objectives and solutions. The League would deemphasize its ambassadorial role, assume the position of facilitator, and empower ghetto blacks. Young never understated the seriousness and depth of racial realities when trying to enlist corporate, government, and foundation assistance in attacking these problems.

Moreover, Young played a key role in organizing black leaders and the groups they represented. With substantial backing from Stephen Currier of the Taconic Foundation and other contributors, Young helped to form the Council for United Civil Rights Leadership (CUCRL). The group consisted of the heads of major civil rights organizations, and they divided funds given to the coalition by several philanthropists. Young also realized that the National Urban League could assist blacks if organizations with similar goals became involved in tackling urban problems. Accordingly, he became a founder of the National Urban Coalition, a group which attempted in 1966 to forge formal alliances between business and government to solve urban ills. Young also reached out to Black Power advocates who espoused racial separatism and physical resistance to white racism. In the late 1960s he helped Imamu Amiri Baraka in efforts to revive Newark, New Jersey, by deepening black participation in the city's political and economic decision making. He endorsed the application of CORE, now a black separatist group, when officials sought foundation funding for a special project in Cleveland. Young never allowed his rapport with powerful whites to undermine his credibility with grassroots black organizations. He wanted blacks who populated the pews of black churches and filled the membership rolls of social, fraternal, professional, and service organizations to ratify his leadership and endorse the interracialism he articulated.

Each of the "Big Six" brought unique contributions and perspectives to the civil rights struggles of the 1950s and 1960s. With his stirring oratory, King drew upon the rich religious and cultural heritage of blacks to articulate in moral and democratic terms their hopes and aspirations. Wilkins used the NAACP's numerous contacts in the White House and in Congress to get important civil rights legislation enacted. Farmer, Lewis, and Forman represented organizations that worked at the grassroots mobilizing blacks to register to vote and urging them to challenge unjust racial practices through sit-ins, freedom rides, and marches. Height injected an organized female presence in a movement largely dependent on women's support, but one in which men held the most visible and influential positions.

Whitney M. Young Jr., alone among these civil rights leaders, drew unprecedented financial support, mainly from foundations and corporations, to the civil rights movement. Although foundations had been involved in racial affairs for several decades, Young persuaded them to give larger amounts to the National Urban League and to other civil rights groups. Also, most businessmen, except for a notable few, had remained aloof from racial betterment organizations. Whitney Young changed that. He persuaded corporate leaders to give substantial contributions to his group, and he involved them more conspicuously in civil rights and urban affairs. He capitalized on his relationships with Presidents Kennedy, Johnson, and Nixon to influence the appointment of blacks to key subcabinet and agency positions within the executive branch and to attract federal money to important League projects.

Young was a pragmatist, an organizer, and a facilitator who built coalitions between factions of black integrationist leaders and later reached out to include younger and more militant Black Power advocates. At the same time, he solidified relationships with corporate leaders and foundation executives and involved them in the civil rights movement. He moved the once conservative National Urban League into the thicket of the black struggles of the 1960s. Moreover, he changed its focus and direction when rioting in major cities and the rise of Black Power convinced him that the League clientele required greater input in the creation and implementation of programs aimed at assisting them. No longer would the organization confine its role to speaking to powerful whites for poor urban blacks. It would now help inner-city residents to design programs and spearhead groups to express their needs and aspirations to white-controlled public and private institutions.

Whitney M. Young Jr. was a mediator between deprived blacks and powerful whites, who tried to reconcile their different perspectives and interests. He also communicated to white Americans the integrationist vision of millions of middle- and working-class blacks who wanted an end to social and economic barriers based on race.

Stokely Carmichael and Black Militancy

Charlie Cobb

Despite a mixed legacy, Stokely Carmichael—or Kwame Ture as he was called later in life—lent a powerful voice to black discontent during the civil rights movement. As a young adult, Carmichael participated in Freedom Rides, interracial bus trips that challenged segregated public transportation, voter registration drives, and many other protest events. Intelligent and highly charismatic, Carmichael was appointed chairman of the Student Nonviolent Coordinating Committee (SNCC). As leader of the SNCC, Carmichael challenged the organization's pacifist agenda and promoted instead a more militant—and provocative—philosophy: black nationalism at any cost. He alienated many followers when he became an outspoken figure in the radical Black Panther Party and later embraced Pan-African causes. The following profile, written by Charlie Cobb, who participated in the civil rights movement alongside Stokely and others, examines Carmichael's evolving ideology and traces his rise to the forefront of the civil rights movement. The article includes portions of an interview with Carmichael before his 1998 death.

🐝 🐝 🐝

Charlie Cobb, "Black Power: A Defiant Young Stokely Carmichael Gave Rise to a Waning Civil Rights Movement and Today's Kwame Ture," *Emerge*, vol. 8, June 30, 1997, p. 38. Copyright © 1997 by Charles Cobb Jr. Reproduced by permission.

Stokely Carmichael's anger boiled over as he spoke to 3,000 people in a park in Greenwood, Miss. "This is the 27th time," he said of his arrest earlier that day. It had been one time too many. "I ain't going to jail no more. . . . We been saying 'Freedom' for six years and we ain't got nothin'. What we gonna start saying now is Black Power!" he roared to amens, applause and stomping feet. He stood, eyes blazing and his finger pointing like a wrathful prophet.

Willie Ricks, a Student Nonviolent Coordinating Committee (SNCC) organizer, leapt to the platform. "BLACK POWER!" Ricks chanted. "What do you want?" he shouted. "BLACK POWER!" the crowd shouted back. "What do you want?" "BLACK POWER!"

In an instant, the smoldering embers of Black nationalism had ignited and North and South connected. In angry Black urban ghettos, young militant Southern civil rights organizers found political soil as fertile as the cotton country where they had faced hostile sheriffs and White Citizens Councils.

That moment on June 16, 1966, has been captured in photographs. And in the minds of many, it is as if Stokely Carmichael has been captured, too, frozen there, forever young, bold and on fire. The popular image is of a militantly anti-White Stokely Carmichael driving the Southern Civil Rights Movement away from the ideals of nonviolence and integration. It's as if Stokely Carmichael not only appeared suddenly before America, but suddenly inside the Civil Rights Movement itself, changing it through the sheer force of his own personality.

But to study the evolution of Stokely Carmichael is to study the evolution of a movement. He did not invent Black Power. He did give it a voice. He rocked America with fiery speeches, angering Whites and some Blacks alike. . . .

Carmichael's Background

The currents that shaped Kwame Ture run deep, and the roots of his political longevity begin first with his family. Neither of his Trinidadian parents finished high school but books filled the shelves in his home. So did talk of independence. Trinidad was still a British colony in the 1950s. His father, a carpenter, believed the United States offered better prospects, and in 1952 at the age of 11, Stokely Carmichael arrived in New York, where he would become a U.S. citizen.

After passing a competitive exam, he entered one of New York City's most elite public high schools: The Bronx High School of Science. An honor student, he devoured books to keep up with his new friends.

He was surprised one day to learn that a White classmate lived in Harlem. "You know I had to go to his house." It turned out that his friend's father was a Communist Party member. "Spending nights there, I met [U.S. Communist Party head] Gus Hall and lots of those folks," he says. But what they offered conflicted with touchstones of Black life. "To be a Marxist-Leninist, you had to be an atheist. I could be an atheist but I knew my people would never tolerate it. And they didn't want any discussion of Black nationalism."

What young Stokely could not find among his White Leftist friends, he found on Harlem street corners: dynamic orations on race and Black nationalist analysis. Bayard Rustin, who was Black and socialist, was crucial. Stokely volunteered in Rustin's office for the youth marches of 1958 and 1959. He finally met Rustin his freshman year in college. "We were at a meeting of White Leftists and Bayard smashed them all. They were talking all of this theory and Bayard said, 'The movement should be guided by serious action, not what you think some book is saying.' I asked, 'Who's he?' and someone said, 'Bayard Rustin.' I said, 'That's who I wanna be!'"

The student sit-ins had begun when Carmichael headed off to Howard University in the fall of 1960. He flourished there intellectually and politically, joining the Nonviolent Action Group (NAG), a tiny activist island in Howard's vast bourgeois sea. Professors, such as Sterling Brown and Harold Lewis, took special interest in the NAG activists. They were their intellectual children and the next generation of "race man." Says Courtland Cox, another SNCC activist, "Sterling would invite us to his house and talk to us about music or Black life in America, and it wasn't a lecture, it was like a conversation."

Carmichael's Influence

Like Stokely, several NAG members, including myself, eventually would make their way South. But even in Stokely's early days at Howard, he showed an instinct for mobilizing people. "He'd say, 'We're going out to demonstrate and afterwards we're going to have a big party," recalls Cox. "And they came out too, these guys who were totally apolitical."

May Lovelace O'Neal traces her activism to Stokely. They met one day when he threw snowballs at her. Soon they were dating. "Carmichael was not my ideal and I was exactly what he didn't want me to be. I was like a cheerleader, a bubble-head; gonna have a husband who is rich and famous, not infamous."

Soon, the Mississippi native became active herself. "I knew all the crap Black people had to live with and it seemed to me that the movement would make it better," says O'Neal, now an art professor at the University of California-Berkeley.

Stokely's freshman year ended in the spring of 1961, the same time that the Congress of Racial Equality (CORE) launched its Freedom Rides in the South. When the first freedom riders were bombed and brutalized, campus groups like NAG believed such violence could not go unchallenged. Stokely was among those who signed up to continue the rides. As a result, he spent 49 days in Mississippi's notorious Parchman Penitentiary that summer. There, he was beaten "all the time." Borrowing from an old song, he told one of his prison tormentors, "I'm gonna tell God how you treat me."

Stokely spent summers in Mississippi until he graduated college in 1964. Then, he went to stay, becoming the SNCC project director for the Second Congressional District, essentially the Mississippi Delta—cotton country, where two-thirds of the population was Black and virtually none was registered to vote.

The bonds formed then between SNCC organizers such as Stokely and older rural Mississippians such as Fannie Lou Hamer went to the heart of SNCC's unique contribution. For all the dangers SNCC workers faced, it was Mississippi's locals who bore the brunt of the violence. It was they who suffered economic reprisals and the terrorizing visits from nightriders. Most of us soon learned that our main challenge was getting Black people to challenge themselves—to have confidence they could stand up and win.

"A large part of the SNCC work . . . was psychological," says Charles Hamilton, a political science professor at Columbia University and co-author of *Black Power* with Stokely. "To get people to believe that they could, at first organize, and then proceed to make a difference in their own lives," was a victory. "And I think those young folks, including Carmichael, were just the ones to do it."

But it was unclear whether the political system was willing to accept meaningful change. The 1964 Mississippi Summer Project—a coordinated effort by all the civil rights organizations, and students from the North, to register voters—sought to answer that question. That

dramatic and tragic summer seemingly gave us the answer. It was the summer that CORE workers James
Chaney, Andrew Goodman and Michael Schwerner
were slain and SNCC workers traveled with members
of the hard-won and newly formed Mississippi Democratic Freedom Party (MDFP) to the Democratic National Convention in Atlantic City, N.J.

Under the banner of the MDFP, the state's Black residents challenged the seating of the all-White regular
Mississippi Party. Critics have characterized this effort
as radical Blacks manipulating uneducated Mississippi
Blacks, but it was the Democrats who turned their
backs on the MDFP.

Although no one disputed that Mississippi Blacks
were systematically denied the right to vote, only the
"regular" party was seated. What happened next turned
disappointment into fury. In their arrogance, the Democrats selected two MDFP members to sit as honorary/
delegates. And as Vice President Hubert Humphrey
was sitting down in a hotel room ostensibly to discuss a

*Stokely Carmichael speaks at Berkeley in 1966, promoting black militancy and
urging activists to fight racism by any means necessary.*

compromise with the delegation leaders, the party's credentials committee and Sen. Walter Mondale announced the "compromise" at a press conference.

The MDFP delegation rejected the offer, despite pressure from liberal allies. It was there that Hamer made her now-famous stand. Asked if the delegation was seeking equality with the White man, Hamer replied. "No. What would I look like fighting for equality with the White man? I don't want to go down that low."

For Stokely, who like the rest of us SNCC organizers had donned jacket and tie to lobby delegates, the convention was a turning point. "I said there that SNCC can no longer go with the Democratic Party," he recalls now.

After Atlantic City, uncertainty hovered over much of our work in the rural counties where we had spent so much time organizing. Few of us were prepared to admit that we didn't know where we were headed. And even within a tightly knit group like SNCC, political fissures began to appear.

When the MDFP decided to continue trying to become a part of the Democratic Party, Stokely disagreed. "It seemed like putting all your eggs in one basket," he says today. "It was clear to me that you needed an independent Black party."

But Lawrence Guyot, who headed the MDFP and had been a SNCC organizer, wasn't ready to give up. "To not fight the Democrats in Mississippi was not to fight segregation. Our position was that SNCC had done a great job organizing but new people were in charge now and SNCC had no more right to control the MDFP than anyone else."

In a sense, Stokely agreed. He announced suddenly that he was leaving Mississippi to work in Alabama's soil-rich blackbelt.

While he and a small band of organizers slipped quietly into Lowndes County, others of us pursued the organizing that we knew how to do, though our vision of where it would lead had been dimmed.

Stokely entered Alabama during the height of King's Selma campaign in March 1965. The Selma-to-Montgomery march seemed an outdated tactic, but its passage through the heart of the predominantly Black county also created political opportunity.

The 1965 Voting Rights Act, passed in the wake of Selma, dramatically began to boost the number of Black registered voters. And a unique Alabama law encouraged creation of county-level political parties. "The law stipulated you had to have a symbol because of the high rate of illiteracy," Ture recalls. "Well, the Democratic Party symbol was a White rooster, the White cock party we used to call it."

Black organizers stumbled upon another symbol.

The Black Panther Party

"Courtland [Cox] came to Atlanta and asked me to design a business card with an emblem for the party," recalls Ruth Howard Chambers, now a teacher in New York City public schools. "I came up with a dove. Nobody thought that worked and someone said I should look at the Clark College [now Clark Atlanta University] emblem. . . . That's where the panther came from." That pouncing Black panther gave instant visibility to the newly formed Lowndes County Freedom Organization as the "Black Panther Party." The slogan: "Power for Black People."

When a volunteer from Oakland, Calif., working in Lowndes County returned home, Huey P. Newton and Bobby Seale asked for permission to use the emblem for a party they were forming.

A year after Stokely's arrival, as the Lowndes County Freedom Organization was selecting candidates, SNCC met outside Nashville, Tenn., to determine its own direction and leader.

Our meetings were chaotic affairs. It was the one place where we could unwind and let down our guard after working in rural pockets filled with fear and hostility. We made decisions by consensus. Often that meant all-nighters. It was in one of these sessions in spring 1966 that Stokely Carmichael was elected SNCC chairman after John Lewis, chairman since 1963, already had been elected hours before.

"It was like a thousand years had passed since 1960," says Ivanhoe Donaldson, a longtime friend and SNCC organizer who worked closely with Stokely in Mississippi. "We were reading [Franz] Fanon not [Albert] Camus. But it wasn't so much about blackness, and Stokely wasn't the purest Black nationalist, anyway. It was about revolution and change and internal frustration within the movement. After all, John believed in empowering the Black community, too. But they had two different personality profiles. John was almost innocent, gentle. Stokely was talking about taking on the country . . . going to the wall."

Says Lewis, now a U.S. congressman from Atlanta, "More than anything else, what happened in 1966 can be traced to what happened in Atlantic City in 1964. Stokely and I were symbols about the sense of direction. . . . I didn't take it personally. Change is bound to come in any movement where you don't have a top-down structure."

Soon SNCC was being increasingly defined by its new chairman as he went from one speaking engagement to another. He was receiving invitations from everywhere. SNCC organizing efforts were slipping. At one point, Cleveland Sellers, elected program secretary at the Tennessee meeting, cabled Stokely in Cuba, asking him to tone down his rhetoric.

At times it could be overwhelming, Hamilton recalls of his friend. Once, while the two worked on their book, says Hamilton, "Stokely came back from answering a call and he said, 'I'm too young for all of this.' I said, 'What do you mean?' He said, 'This is all happening too fast. I need time to grow and think'. . . . He was 24. I thought that was a very mature response."

Indeed, his life was moving fast. He joined the Black Panther Party, attracted by its confrontations with police and thinking that allying SNCC's veteran rural organizers with urban militants could advance the Black struggle. "Although Black power was born in the South, there's no question that the urban rebellions gave it its force," says Ture. It wasn't long, however, before he was feeling the pressure many Panthers felt. But "ill-prepared leadership," and other roiling conflicts inside the party "made it impossible for me to stay," Ture says now. "We even had to duck FBI bullets inside the party."

In the midst of it all, Stokely Carmichael took his first trip to Africa. It was 1967, and Stokely met Ghanaian President Kwame Nkrumah. Brash as ever, though awed at meeting Nkrumah, a personal as well as political hero, he urged Nkrumah, who had been ousted in a military coup and was living in Guinea, to take back Ghana through armed struggle.

"Nkrumah sat me down and asked me why I was so impatient. I told him because I see my people suffering. Well, he asked me, if I saw a boat coming while I was on land, would I wade out and meet it? I said, 'Yes, without question.' He said, 'You'll only get wet and the boat won't come in any faster. The revolution is going to triumph,' he told me. Then he asked me if I thought the revolution would triumph. I said, 'Yes, sir.' 'Oh, I see,' he said. 'It's just that you want to be the one to bring it about. All impatience is selfishness and egotism.'"

It took Stokely two years to get back to Africa. In the

interim, he also visited Vietnam and Cuba, which gave the U.S. government a chance to take his passport and the FBI additional incentive to track his every move.

When he was able to return, Nkrumah suggested that he stay in Africa as his political secretary. Stokely eagerly accepted. In 1969, he moved to Conakry, 'where he heads the All African Peoples Revolutionary Party founded by Nkrumah. He is also on the executive committee of now-deceased Guinean President Sekou Ture's Democratic Party of Guinea. "Only a strong Africa will give us the strength to free ourselves," he says.

His decision to live in Africa brought various reactions, ranging from feelings of abandonment to shock. . . .

SNCC never argued over Pan Africanism. By the time Stokely left for Africa, SNCC had ceased to exist in everything but name. Under his successor, H. Rap Brown, SNCC seemed more militant, and indeed its words were. But grass-roots organizing had stopped. SNCC's reason for being had gone.

And Stokely Carmichael had become Kwame Ture.

Bayard Rustin: Strategist and Tactician

Steven Steinberg

Bayard Rustin was an incontestable figure in the battle for African American rights. A committed activist and master tactician on the protest front, Rustin was a strategic force behind many civil rights struggles, including the Montgomery bus boycott and the March on Washington. He is perhaps best known for his work alongside Martin Luther King Jr. The following profile of Rustin by Steven Steinberg details the formative influences and pivotal events that molded Rustin into a "political gadfly who, more than any other single person, was a catalyst behind the various stages of the evolving civil rights movement." In his recounting, Steinberg includes Rustin's metamorphosis from a civil rights protester to a political figure. This career turn catapulted Rustin, the once consummate activist, into the political center—a move that prompted some to conclude that he had softened his stance on racial issues, thereby abandoning some of the ideals upon which his early career was founded. Steinberg contributed the following article to *New Politics*.

🐝 🐝 🐝

Steven Steinberg, "Bayard Rustin and the Rise and Decline of the Black Protest Movement," *New Politics*, vol. 6, Summer 1997. Copyright © 1997 by New Politics Publishing Co. Reproduced by permission.

Rustin is to be remembered as a political gadfly who, more than any other single person, was a catalyst behind the various stages of the civil rights movement as it evolved from individual acts of resistance, to fledgling organizations that forged a praxis for challenging the Jim Crow system in the South, to a full-fledged political movement that not only overcame seemingly insuperable odds to achieve its immediate objectives, but also ushered in a period of extraordinary progressive transformation. This is Bayard Rustin's incontestable political legacy. . . .

Formative Years

Rustin was raised in West Chester, Pennsylvania, by his maternal grandmother, who was a Quaker in her youth, and became a charter member of the NAACP in 1910. These two political strains—pacifism and racial activism were to become the leitmotif of Rustin's life, though as we shall see, they at times coalesced into a potent amalgam but at other times were fatally at odds with one another.

Rustin's career as political activist began in high school when he was arrested for refusing to sit in the balcony of the local moviehouse, dubbed Nigger Heaven. As offensive lineman on the football team, he instigated a revolt among his black teammates to their Jim Crow accommodations. He led a group of classmates in acts of defiance to Jim Crow practices in restaurants, soda fountains, movie houses, department stores, and the YMCA. Graduating with honors in 1932, Rustin was class valedictorian and received a prize for excellence in public speaking. If this were the first act of a play, one would applaud the playwright for skillfully weaving together the various elements of personality and intellect that would drive the narrative.

Rustin did two short stints at black colleges, Wilberforce and Cheyney State Teachers College. In the spring of 1937, he returned to Cheyney for a two-week training program as a peace volunteer, sponsored by the American Friends Service Committee. Here peace volunteers were trained in the tactics of opposing war with courage and goodwill, and then dispatched to towns and cities across America. That winter Rustin abruptly packed his bags and moved to Harlem, where he lived with his aunt, a public-school teacher, on Sugar Hill. The Communist Party had a conspicuous presence in Harlem. As Rustin would comment later, it was the one organized group speaking out about the Scottsboro case and the ravages of Jim Crow in the South. It was apparently at the behest of the Young Communist League [YCL] that Rustin enrolled as a student at CCNY [City College of New York] in 1938. There he played a leading role in the Communist takeover of the student senate, its campus newspaper, and the American Student Union. In 1941 the YCL commissioned Rustin to organize a campaign against segregation in the armed forces, but that directive was abruptly withdrawn when the Nazis invaded the Soviet Union in June 1941. Disillusioned, Rustin quit the YCL, and on that very day walked down the hill into A. Philip Randolph's office. In short order Rustin was assigned to head the youth arm of Randolph's emerging March on Washington Movement (MOWM).

According to [Rustin biographer Jervis] Anderson, Rustin registered "explosive dissent" at Randolph's decision to call off the march after Roosevelt issued his executive order desegregating defense industries. He and other "radical youth organizers" were also disappointed that no concessions had been won concerning the desegregation of the armed forces. With the MOWM in remission, Rustin shifted his allegiances to the pacifist movement, and began working for the Fellowship of Reconciliation (FOR). As field secretary for youth and general affairs, Rustin crisscrossed the country, organizing new chapters, lecturing on college campuses, addressing civic and religious groups—in short, honing his skills as a political organizer.

FOR was a breeding ground for radical ideas and leaders, most of whom were disciples of Mahatma Gandhi. With James Farmer as its race relations secretary and Rustin as field secretary, FOR was the progenitor of the Congress of Racial Equality [CORE], founded in 1940 with Rustin as its first field secretary. CORE combined the racial militancy of Randolph's MOWM with the tactics of the pacifist movement, thus forging a new praxis, centered around nonviolent direct action, for challenging Jim Crow in the South. Although CORE's experiments with sit-ins and boycotts were minimally effective in the 1940s, they constituted a political legacy that was readily adopted by the evolving civil rights movement in the 1950s.

As a conscientious objector, Rustin was exempted from the draft on the condition that he enlist in the Civilian Public Service. He refused. Like the radical activists in the War Resisters League, Rustin regarded the civilian work camps as aiding the war effort, and he was sentenced to three years in a federal prison. There he joined other conscientious objectors in hunger strikes against segregated seating in the dining hall.

Emerging from prison in June 1946, Rustin went back to work for the Fellowship of Reconciliation as race relations secretary, a position that he shared with George Houser. Together they planned a Journey of Reconciliation to demand enforcement of a recent Supreme Court ruling against Jim Crow in interstate buses. Thurgood Marshall warned that a "disobedience movement on the part of Negroes and their white allies, if employed in the South, would result in wholesale slaughter with no good achieved." Marshall was not entirely wrong, at least measured by the short term. Rustin narrowly escaped violence, was arrested and sentenced to a harrowing 22 days on a chain gang, and the buses remained segregated. On the other hand, the Journey was a precursor to the freedom rides of the 1960s. As Rustin commented in 1948: "the Journey of Reconciliation was organized not only to devise techniques for eliminating Jim Crow in travel, but also as a training ground for similar peaceful projects against discrimination in such major areas as employment and in the armed services." Rustin's political genius was his ability to simultaneously pursue short-term and long-term objectives, without allowing one to eclipse the other.

It is noteworthy that Rustin's activism on behalf of civil rights was grounded in a broader matrix of ideological principles, and his activism found varied outlets. Indeed, Rustin was the peripatetic organizer who over a lifetime of activism would gravitate to whatever struggle emerged for peace, democracy, or racial justice. In 1946 he travelled to India to meet with Gandhi intellectuals, stopping in Britain to address various pacifist groups. Then he worked for several years in a campaign against America's development of nuclear weapons and its programs for war preparedness. Soon after the abortive Journey of Reconciliation he travelled to Paris and Moscow with David Dellinger and other pacifists. In Paris he learned about the emerging anticolonial struggles in Africa, and in 1952 travelled to Africa on a mission sponsored by the Fellowship of Reconciliation and the American Friends Service Committee, with the purpose of linking American pacifist movement with leaders of West African independence. After a humiliating arrest for a homosexual incident in 1953, he was ejected from the Fellowship of Reconciliation. But a year later he was appointed executive secretary of the

War Resisters League, a position that he retained for 12 years, though he was frequently "released" to work with the evolving civil rights movement.

The Montgomery Bus Boycott

Rustin's rendezvous with destiny came in December 1955, when Rosa Parks's act of courage precipitated the Montgomery bus boycott which would catapult Martin Luther King into a leadership position. By February Rustin was summoned to Montgomery. At 44 he was a seasoned organizer; King, at 27, was a neophyte who by sheer accident was drawn into the swirling vortex of black revolt. King had previous academic exposure to Gandhi, but according to Anderson, it was Rustin who prevailed on King to dispense with armed guards and to embrace nonviolent action as the trademark of the budding movement. It was also Rustin who forged links to radicals in the North. In April 1956 *Liberation* carried King's first piece of political journalism, and Rustin and the War Resisters League mobilized leading pacifists and radicals into a Committee for Nonviolent Integration which funneled aid to King. Rustin helped to organize yet another group, In Friendship, which sponsored a rally at Madison Square Garden that raised some $20,000 for the Montgomery Improvement Association. There was always nervousness among King's advisors about Rustin's Communist past and his homosexuality, but his organizing skills and political savvy proved indispensable.

It would be difficult to exaggerate Rustin's contribution as the Montgomery boycott evolved into a broad strategy for protest. According to Anderson, Rustin "conceived and charted" the Southern Christian Leadership Conference, along with Ella Baker and Stanley Levison. This was to serve as the organizational mechanism for King's ascent to national prominence. Over the next decade Rustin remained a close advisor to King, especially during moments of crisis. Rustin was the chief organizer of the Prayer Pilgrimage—a precursor to the March on Washington. Held at the Lincoln Memorial on the third anniversary of the Brown decision, the Pilgrimage drew some 30,000 participants from labor, student, religious, and civil rights organizations. This was King's first major protest event outside the South, and his oratorical gifts captured the attention of commentators both inside and outside the movement. Rustin also had a hand in drafting King's first book, *Stride Toward Freedom*, which reached a national audience with the riveting story of the Montgomery boycott. In 1958 Rustin organized yet another mass demonstration in Washington—the Youth March for Integrated Schools. These were the feats of creative organizing through which the civil rights movement grew from a regional protest against Jim Crow to a national movement for racial justice.

Again it is noteworthy, especially as a foreshadow of Rustin's later deviation, that even during this period of heightened racial conflict, Rustin never abandoned his pacifist crusade. As Anderson put it, Rustin was "a leading member of the radical jet set," flying off to conferences in Europe, India, and Africa. In late 1959 Rustin was abroad protesting France's first nuclear test in the Sahara, and was absent from the planning for the 1960 national conventions, much to the ire of Randolph. According to Anderson, "Rustin therefore found himself in the middle of a tug-of-war between the two political causes to which he was equally committed, pacifism and black protest activism."

The March on Washington
Yet it was Bayard Rustin who emerged as the chief organizer and tactician for the climactic 1963 March on

Washington. Despite the qualms of some civil rights leaders, Rustin was named Randolph's deputy director. The march was originally conceived, not as a demonstration for civil rights, but as a demonstration around economic issues, particularly the need for jobs and a higher minimum wage. It was to be sponsored by the Negro American Labor Council, the association of black trade unionists that Randolph formed within the AFL-CIO. According to an internal memorandum that Rustin prepared for Randolph, the march would entail "the co-ordinated participation of all progressive sectors of the liberal, labor, religious, and Negro communities." It was King who insisted that the march focus on civil rights as well as economic issues, and to appease King the march was renamed as a March on Washington for Jobs and Freedom.

The March is remembered as the epitome of protest

Bayard Rustin was one of the chief organizers of the 1963 March on Washington, where thousands of people gathered to peacefully demand civil rights.

politics. It was, after all, "the biggest, and surely the most diverse, demonstration in history for human rights." In retrospect, however, the March was the glorious finale of the protest movement, and embodied the seeds of an imminent transformation "from protest to politics," for Rustin personally and for the movement as a whole.

There was a political price to the coalition that Rustin so actively sought. In order to enlist the support of hundreds of civic, labor, and religious organizations, the politics of the march had to be confined to what was politically safe. As Milton Viorst comments in *Fire in the Streets*, "the March increasingly adopted the posture of a moral witness against evil; participation became not a matter of politics but of conscience, and support swelled."

Thus, while the March had all of the earmarks of "protest," it actually represented the ascendancy of a new brand of "coalition politics," the antithesis of the politics of confrontation that were at the core of the black protest movement. Nothing better illustrates this than the well-documented muzzling of John Lewis. According to Viorst:

> Lewis had planned to denounce Kennedy's civil rights bill as inadequate, and declare that SNCC could not support it. He saw an opportunity for SNCC to shatter an illusion that the palliatives of liberal America could achieve the goals of racial justice. SNCC's rhetoric was now of revolution.

Rustin required all speakers to hand in the text of their speeches the night before, and Lewis's touched off an acrimonious debate. James Forman, who helped draft the speech, insisted that it was "a dynamite speech" that "would puncture the tranquility of the march and the efforts of the Kennedy administration to make this look like a popular uprising in favor of his civil rights bill." On the other hand, Robert Kennedy and Burke Marshall were determined that Lewis be muzzled, and they enlisted the support of Bishop Patrick O'Doyle who was scheduled to deliver the opening invocation. Even as the ceremonies were about to begin, O'Doyle threatened to withdraw. At a hasty conference behind the Lincoln Memorial, Randolph and Rustin prevailed on Lewis to excise the controversial passages.

Thus did a mass demonstration at the apex of the black revolt against America's racial tyranny proceed without so much as a discordant note that might rankle the political establishment. King's celebrated I-have-a-dream oration was embraced precisely because it vented no anger, cast no aspersions, but on the contrary, invoked America's ideals and substituted utopian reverie for political action. It is worth noting that King's oration had another message: "There will be neither rest nor tranquility in America until the Negro is granted his citizenship rights. The whirlwinds of revolt will continue to shake the foundations of our nation until the bright day of justice emerges." But if these words were heard at all, they were instantly expunged from collective memory.

After King spoke, it was Rustin who took the microphone, asking for verbal ratification of the goals of the March: passage of Kennedy's civil rights bill, a $2.00 minimum wage, desegregation of schools, a federal public-works job program, and federal action to bar racial discrimination in employment. Later that evening Rustin and the other civil rights leaders were received at the White House, remuneration for keeping within the bounds of political acceptability. . . .

A Political Centrist
According to Anderson, in the aftermath of the March Rustin "began emerging as a political figure in his own

right, not simply an intellectual factotum of the protest movement." No longer the outsider, the gadfly, the troublemaker, he was photographed alongside Randolph on the cover of *Life*. Whether such personal blandishments played a role in Rustin's move toward the respectable center is difficult to say. What is clear, though, is that the 1963 March marked a decisive turn in Rustin's politics. It would be followed in short order by three events that would complete his political metamorphosis:

1. At the 1964 Democratic National Convention Rustin was drawn into the imbroglio over the challenge by the Mississippi Freedom Democratic Party, organized by SNCC, to unseat the party regulars. At Johnson's behest, Walter Reuther and Hubert Humphrey brokered a compromise that would have given the FDP two seats alongside white supremacists in the Mississippi delegation. Rustin opted on the side of compromise. This, from the man whose credo as both pacifist and civil rights activist was *never* to forego principle for expediency, *never* to back down even if one had to endure the blows and the retribution of the oppressor. . . .

2. Rustin's next act of political perfidy took the form of an article that he published in the February 1965 issue of *Commentary*. Aptly entitled "From Protest to Politics," the article was a manifesto in reverse. Now that the structure of segregation had been destroyed, Rustin reasoned, the politics of confrontation had outlived its purpose. Future progress would depend not on the tactics of direct action, but forging a progressive coalition that would seek power through the Democratic Party. . . .

3. The third and least explicable act of political perfidy was when Rustin became an apologist for Johnson's Vietnam policy. Anderson puts a sympathetic spin on it: "his new role in the building of coalition

politics had helped him to recognize that absolute pacifism was no longer politically effective." Needless to say, Rustin's erstwhile allies in the pacifist movement were outraged when Rustin echoed the Administration's line on Vietnam. . . .

The early Bayard Rustin remains an inspirational figure, all the more so at a time when the radical tide is in such low ebb. According to Lerone Bennett . . . the black revolt failed in each decade only to reemerge on a higher level of development. Rustin's example testifies to why this is so. Because there are people in the trenches who keep the radical faith. Who are there to resuscitate flagging movements. Who function as purveyors of radical ideas and a radical praxis, even at times when their impact is minimal. Who develop incisive and uncompromising critiques of the political establishment. Who place honesty and principle above winning elections. And who are there when . . . when the conditions are ripe for radical ascendancy.

This is the lesson to be drawn from Bayard Rustin's remarkable personal odyssey: to stay the course even when the radical tide is in low ebb. There is also a lesson to be drawn from Rustin's political fall: to resist the blandishments of power during those rare moments of radical ascendancy.

Fannie Lou Hamer: Unlikely Heroine

Kay Mills

Although poor and uneducated, Fannie Lou Hamer emerged as one of the most eloquent speakers for the civil rights movement. A sharecropper, Hamer spent much of her life in the rural South, where—like other southern blacks— she was subjected to brutalizing Jim Crow laws. In one harrowing incident, Hamer was jailed, brutally beaten, and fired from her job for attempting to register to vote. In response, Hamer entered the political arena. Despite her lack of formal education, the fiercely resolute Hamer spoke out on myriad civil rights issues, most notably voting rights, and worked with various grassroots organizations. She is perhaps best known for her affiliation with the Student Nonviolent Coordinating Committee (SNCC), an organization that promoted peaceful social protest as a response to racial strife. The following selection is excerpted from *This Little Light of Mine: The Life of Fannie Lou Hamer* by Kay Mills.

❦ ❦ ❦

Fannie Lou Hamer was poor and unlettered. She walked with a limp. A short, stocky black woman, for much of her life she worked weighing the cotton picked on a white man's plantation in the heart of the Mississippi Delta. She lived in a small frame house that had no hot water and no working indoor toilet—while her boss's dog had its own bathroom inside the main house. She had an earthy sense of humor, an ability to quote vast passages from the Bible, and the respect of those who knew her. They counted on her to straighten out disputes and intercede in the white community when necessary and knew that she and her husband, Pap, would take in children other families could not raise. She knew there was much wrong with America, but until the civil rights movement came to her town, she could do little about those wrongs.

The summer that the movement reached Fannie Lou Hamer's hometown of Ruleville—1962—she was forty-four years old, and she could not vote. She wanted that right, and in her struggle to achieve it she became a symbolic figure who inspired countless other Americans, those who met her and many who never did. Like many Delta blacks, she lived for a time a life of resignation, making the best of what she had and trying to enjoy her family and her friends. But she was ready when a movement came to Mississippi that could match her mountainous talents.

Voting Rights

Mississippi and other southern states had effectively taken the vote from their black citizens by requiring them to pass a test to register, one they almost always failed because it was administered by people who did not want them to pass. A black person too well educated to be denied the right to register was often forced to choose between voting only for white candidates or not voting at all.

The intimidation was usually economic. The few

good jobs that black people could get in rural Mississippi were as teachers in the all-black school system. A white board of education and a white superintendent controlled all teaching jobs. Most black people picked cotton or cleaned and cooked for white people. They may have rebelled in their own private ways—spitting in the soup is a favorite tale—but most dared not speak out. The only people with any measure of independence were black preachers and funeral directors; many of them squandered even that minimal independence by currying favor with whites.

Those who found neither outright exploitation nor indirect subservience palatable left Mississippi for East St. Louis, the South Side of Chicago, Gary, or Detroit. Those who demanded fair treatment at home often were forced to head north as well or risk joining the ranks of the lynched. The trees and bayous of the Delta are often the only features on the flat landscape; they also served as the tools of repression when blacks were hanged or dumped off a bridge, never to be seen alive again. Fannie Lou Hamer knew all these landmarks only too well. The cruelty of the Delta was only part of white supremacist violence that marked Mississippi as the most repressive state of the South.

By almost any measure, black Mississippians had little share in the American Dream of opportunity as they entered the 1960s. The focus of early organizing drives in the Delta was the right to vote—but few could worry about voting when there were almost no jobs left picking cotton and no proper schooling to qualify a black person for whatever jobs did exist. Few could worry about voting when children went hungry and rain poured through holes in the roof, or when children died in fires caused by primitive stoves in unheated shacks. Or when people went to the hospital only to die. Or when the white world was deliberately leaving blacks further behind, and when its rear guard of white sheriffs turned their dogs on those trying to assert their rights, and men riding at night fired shotguns at them or tried to burn down their barns. A few black southerners like Medgar Evers had braved the night, too, signing people up for the National Association for the Advancement of Colored People, trying to get people to vote, resisting this violent system even before Dr. Martin Luther King, Jr. burst into the headlines with his leadership of the Montgomery, Alabama, bus boycott.

There were thus a handful of people, but only that, ready to hear the message of the young civil rights workers when they arrived in Ruleville in August 1962. The workers called their gatherings "mass meetings" for psychological reasons, but sometimes the mass was fairly small. They met at a church because that was the only place a gathering of black people wouldn't arouse whites' suspicions. In between the singing, they would preach. Their message was one of hope and faith— hope that people would hear their words about the value of voting, faith that they would be sufficiently brave to make the word deed. Then they asked who would go with them to try to register. Fannie Lou Hamer put up her hand. That night she changed her own destiny and that of a great many others, black and white. She would lose her job, be jailed and beaten, for her beliefs. She symbolized one aspect of what the movement hoped to accomplish: to embolden local people to resist a harsh and violent system.

Hamer's Activism

From this humblest of beginnings, Mrs. Hamer would go on to challenge the president of the United States, the national Democratic Party, members of Congress, and the American people about fulfilling the promises of democracy. She recognized the shortcomings in the nation's electoral and educational systems. She opposed the war in Vietnam from the beginning, and she was thrilled by seeing Africans govern themselves. She organized programs to feed poor people, tend to their ills, house them, clothe them, train them for jobs. She ran for office. She recognized the need for women of all races to work together for political and social goals. She encouraged young people to set and achieve their own goals.

She was not some ethereal being who lived unscathed amid poverty. Her health and formal education were severely stunted by her surroundings; her penetrating analysis of society was at times dismissed by those who picked apart her unlettered grammar or could hear only her Delta dialect. She was thoroughly human: she snored, she cracked earthy jokes, she mimicked bigoted people. She understood the fears held by violent whites—suffered as a result of them—but she did not hate them for she was a true Christian. She often was undiplomatic: she could flay a public official or those less resolute than she on a moment's notice. She was not perfect, but she was, to many who worked with her under the most life-threatening conditions, the most inspirational person they ever knew. They drew from her and Mississippians like her a self-confidence that helped them later in facing their own difficulties, achieving their own successes.

She died poor because she gave away much of what she earned or raised. She thought she was dying forgotten because few people visited her during the debilitating illnesses of her last years, and because many turned away from her when she no longer had money or energy to give to their needs. Yet more people who had been active in the movement, famous and unknown, turned out for her funeral than she ever realized honored and revered her.

Roy Wilkins and the NAACP

Joe Johnson

Roy Wilkins's passionate commitment to civil rights commenced early in life: As a college student, Wilkins joined the National Association for the Advancement of Colored People (NAACP) and participated in many demonstrations and other events that promoted interracial equality. Having established himself as a highly articulate spokesperson for civil rights, Wilkins was appointed executive secretary of the NAACP in 1955. Throughout his twenty-two year career with the NAACP, Wilkins tirelessly advocated protest and resistance as tools to dismantle racism and empower African Americans. At the same time, he remained a steadfast proponent of a multiracial society, speaking out against the separatist credo of more militant civil rights leaders. The following article by Joe Johnson originally appeared in the NAACP's publication, *Crisis*. In describing Wilkins's life and legacy, Johnson examines the forces that shaped the civil rights activist into a "towering figure" in American history.

❧   ❧   ❧

Joe Johnson, "Roy Wilkins," *The Crisis*, January 1988, p. 26. Copyright © 1988 by The Crisis Publishing Company, Inc. Reproduced by permission of the publisher and the author. The publisher wishes to thank The Crisis Publishing Co., the publisher of the magazine of the National Association for the Advancement of Colored People, for the use of this material first published in the January 1988 issue of *The Crisis*.

Roy Wilkins was a towering figure because his work embraced the aspirations and struggle of Afro-American people for freedom and empowerment through protest. Key to understanding the contributions of Roy Wilkins is understanding his vision and the forces that molded him.

Once, reminiscing about the tradition of his personal legacy of protest and resistance, Roy Wilkins called on the memory of his father:

> My father had enough education to realize that the equality of all men as set forth in the Declaration of Independence wasn't exactly common policy around Marshall County [Mississippi]; he became the family's first hell-raiser. Since he talked back to white people whenever he felt like it, people around Holly Springs began to worry about him. They said he was on his way to becoming a troublemaker, bum, and all-around bad nigger. I have the same traits buried somewhere in my chromosomes. I don't like to be mistreated. I believe in fighting back.

This tradition of fight-back led to William Wilkins, Roy's father, trouncing a bigot who threatened his life. As a consequence of William Wilkins' militancy, he fled Mississippi to avoid a lynch mob. "The Lord may have delivered Daniel from the lion's den and Grandfather Wilkins from slavery, but it was the Illinois Central that delivered my father from Mississippi—one step ahead of the lynch mob," Roy Wilkins later wrote.

Shortly after his father's exodus from rural Mississippi to St. Louis, Missouri, Roy was born in 1901. Although thoroughly segregated, St. Louis offered more possibility than the rural south. But when Roy was four, the Wilkinses' limited tranquility was shattered by his mother's premature death. Unable to manage the burden of three young children, William Wilkins strongly considered the possibility of sending his children to his parents in Mississippi, but Roy's maternal aunt, Elizabeth Williams, intervened. With the consent of Roy's father, the children were taken to St Paul, Minnesota. Thus, within his brief life span, Roy Wilkins confronted the death of his mother and the fear of his family dissolving. Life demanded that the boy absorb the tragedy and move on.

Fortunately, Roy, his sister Armenda and his brother Earl found the shelter and security in the home of his maternal aunt Elizabeth and her husband Samuel. The children had the advantage of the strong example of love and hard work shown daily in their interactions with their Aunt Elizabeth and Uncle Samuel. Observing his Uncle Sam handle a grueling schedule of hard, menial work with dignity, Roy found a lifelong role model. "He was the warmest, kindest man I have ever met. Over the years he taught me that the world was not a universally hostile place my father had taken it to be; that a man could get along if he had faith in the goodness of other people, kept his eye peeled for their weaknesses, and believed in himself. Everything I am or hope to be I owe to him."

An Integrated Society

In addition to helping the Wilkins children adjust to the loss of their mother and father, the St. Paul experience shaped Roy's vision about the possibilities of an American society where people with common goals and different backgrounds work and live together in harmony and respect. In St. Paul, Minnesota, Roy Wilkins experienced a functioning integrated society, where the worth of an individual was valued over his/her skin color:

> I suppose the faith I have in integration comes from the days I spent in a schoolboy's cap and knickers chasing around the quiet tree-shaded lanes that stretched off and away from our little cottage. The

men who owned the tidy frame houses in my neighborhood were white: Swedes and Norwegians, Poles,
Germans, and Irish—first and second generation
immigrants. They worked as carpenters, patching up
boxcars in the nearby yards of the Northern Pacific,
or as laborers and janitors, watchmen, policemen,
and firemen. I don't remember any rich people living in our part of town.

Separatism Versus Integration

This integrated social interaction was valuable in forming visions about the possibility of interracial cooperation and harmony:

> Perhaps I'm a sentimentalist, but no one can tell me
> that it is impossible for white people and black
> people to live next door to one another, to get
> along—even to love one another. For me, integra-
> tion is not an abstraction constructed on dusty eigh-
> teenth century notions of democracy. I believe in it,
> not only because it is right, but because I have lived
> it all my life.

For Wilkins, this was an enduring experience. . . .

When the doctrine of black power separatism appeared in the 60s, it challenged Wilkins' concept of the
multi-cultural society and the strategic goal of the
NAACP to attain an integrated society. Thus, the call
for separatism by Stokely Carmichael, H. Rap Brown,
and other black student leaders was an anathema. According to Wilkins, "Racial segregation, preached and
urged by a youthful minority of Negro Americans, can
be the means of plunging their race back behind the
barbed wire of restriction, inferiority, persecution and
death to both the spirit and the body. The black youth
of today owe it to themselves to study the appalling ef-
fects of segregation. When one asks for a little bit of it
in order to go off in a corner and counsel together, one
asks for the whole bit."

The Power of Racism

But if Wilkins' sensibility was molded by integration, it was also conditioned by segregation. In 1920 while a student at the University of Minnesota, an incident occurred that altered Roy Wilkins' consciousness. A white Minnesota mob stormed a jail, and dragged out three black circus workers who had been accused of assaulting a white woman. The mob lynched the men. "I lost my innocence on race once and for all." For Wilkins this was an important lesson in the vicious power of racism:

> I was just short of nineteen the night that the bodies of McGhee, Jackson, and Clayton swung from a light pole in Duluth. I read the stories in the newspapers and put them down feeling sick, scared and angry all at the same time. This was Minnesota, not Mississippi, but every Negro in the John Robinson Show had been suspect in the eyes of the police and guilty in the eyes of the mob. What bothered me was the way those 5,000 white Northerners had gotten together on the lynching. The mob was in touch with something—an awful hatred I had never seen or felt before. For the first time in my life I had understood what DuBois had been writing about. I found myself thinking of black people as a very vulnerable "us"— and white people as an unpredictable, violent "them."

Later after graduating from college, Wilkins plunged into the politics of race and journalism as editor of the *St. Paul Appeal*, where he increased circulation and improved the news content. Consequently, Wilkins' skill and talent came to the attention of Chester Franklin, an influential black publisher, who offered young Roy a spot on the *Kansas City Call*. By accepting the offer, Wilkins was extending his influence as a crack journalist and activist. His activism took the form of crusades against the racist politicians. From his editor's desk, Wilkins observed the hard, low game of big city racist politics. While editor of the *Call*, Wilkins developed an advocacy column—"*Talking It Over*"—that challenged white intolerance as well as black complacency. Years later, Wilkins commented on his experience as a young journalist in Kansas City: "Kansas ate my heart out. It was a melodramatic thing. It was a slow accumulation of humiliations and grievances. I was constantly exposed to Jim Crow in the schools, movies, downtown hotels and restaurants."

By blending his skills with his passionate concern about the political condition of black Americans, Roy Wilkins' vision matured. This was an important point in Wilkins' ideological development. Because Wilkins experienced the positive social environment of blacks and whites with similar goals and aspirations in St. Paul, Minnesota, the unnatural treatment of blacks in a racist segregated America disturbed him. Consequently, it was no surprise that during the early days as a journalist in Kansas City, Wilkins was both the secretary of the Urban League and the NAACP. It was Walter White, the secretary of the NAACP, who recognized Wilkins' leadership potential, so in 1931 White offered the young editor a position. After receiving the offer, Wilkins expressed his feeling:

> I read the letter several times, my heart thumping. This was no invitation to bury myself in the business department of *The Crisis*, but an offer to work side by side with the most exciting civil rights leaders of the day. I pulled out my typewriter and tapped out a two-paragraph reply. Anything overeager, I cautioned myself, might spoil my chances.
>
> Dear Walter:
> I thank you very much for your letter on February 26. You may say to your committee on administration that I am interested and would be pleased to have it submit its proposal to the board of directors on March 9.
> I want to assure you that I consider it an honor to

be approached with this offer. It seems wise to me to reserve any further discussion until a conference can be held.

Cordially,
Roy

Recognizing the promise and the skills that Wilkins possessed, the NAACP board hired him.

For Wilkins joining the NAACP family at that point in its development was indeed exciting as well as demanding. Under the spiritual and intellectual guidance of one of its founders, W.E.B. DuBois, and the energetic, practical leadership of Walter White, the NAACP campaigned by lobbying presidents, legislators, national leaders, and makers of public opinion to rid America of its Jim Crow ethic and to put an end to the heinous crime of lynching. During the 20's and 30's, this organizational goal demanded all of the NAACP's energy and efforts. In this climate of militant activistism, Wilkins found an ideological home. Using Walter White as an example, Roy Wilkins investigated injustice and exploitation at first hand. By examining the abysmal conditions of black Mississippi workers during the 30's, Wilkins' report—"Mississippi Slave Labor"—led to congressional action to improve working conditions. Wilkins was making a mark as both activist and writer.

Roy Wilkins

When DuBois resigned as editor of *The Crisis* Wilkins assumed the editorship of *The Crisis* issuing in a different ideological point of view. As a result of the shift in editorial point of view, Wilkins made a suggestion to the board: "I suggested that we move away from the magazine's lofty, ebony tower approach and broaden the appeal, audience, and circulation. As a small contribution . . . I wrote my article, about a black sports figure, and they suddenly found themselves in the pages of *The Crisis*, tucked among the most august literary and sociological thinkers of the race. I saw this as an improvement, and whatever Dr. DuBois thought, he kept to himself and graciously printed the story." In addition to broadening the ideological base of *The Crisis*, Wilkins was instrumental in developing the ideological strategy of the NAACP's march to battle the legal obstacles that prevented blacks from enjoying full participation within American society.

Wilkins's Leadership Style

Generally, Wilkins was characterized as a quiet leader. This was a misconception, given the fire and intensity of his writing and his administrative energies. But Wilkins' character fits his role as leader. In an insightful comment about himself, Wilkins remarked:

> I don't remember many children on Laclede [childhood home in St. Louis]; most of the time I played by myself. Even then I was a loner, and I have stayed a loner all my life. I'm not particularly proud of this trait—it can make a man seem a little distant or even aloof—but it has helped pull me through some tight spots and hard times.

Perhaps this loner quality was the right mix for the leadership of a major strategic organization. As one of the important architects, Wilkins' style and skill were considerably balanced for his goal. Wilkins saw his role clearly and realistically:

> The Negro has to be a superb diplomat and a great strategist. He has to parlay what actual power he has along with good will on the white majority. He has

to devise and pursue those philosophies and activities which will least alienate the white majority opinion. And that doesn't mean that the Negro has to indulge in bootlicking, but he must gain the sympathy of the large majority of the American public. He must also seek to make an identification with American tradition.

Part of Wilkins' definition of the American tradition was the tradition of protest. It was this strategy that finally led to the 1954 Supreme Court decision that overturned the doctrine of separate but equal facilities in public education. Wilkins thought of the victory as a team effort. According to Wilkins, "After assaulting segregation in schools and universities, we finally got rid of the dual constitutionality of the separate but equal education concept." For Wilkins, the voting rights, housing, and job opportunity cases followed. His life's work to desegregate the society was approaching fruition. On the other hand, there was another major movement aground, the black power movement. Wilkins responded:

> Black power is the father of hatred and mother of violence. Black power, in the quick, uncritical and highly emotional adoption it has received from the same segments of a beleaguered people, can mean only black death. Even if it should be enthroned briefly, the human spirit would die a little.

The Black Power concept was counter to Wilkins' credo. Wilkins conceived of the civil rights movement as a means to integrate the morality of America. Coupled with his political activism and the organizational goal of the NAACP, Wilkins saw his life's work and the struggle of the black people to gain their rights as a test for the spirit of America:

> Without us, without our struggle, the country would have foundered in moral emptiness long ago. We

must never lose faith in the justness of our cause and the certainty of our success. We have tried to create a nation where all men would be equal in the eyes of the law; where all citizens would be judged on their own ability, not their race. We have believed in our Constitution. We have believed that the Declaration of Independence meant what it said. All my life I have believed these things, and I will die believing them. I share this faith with others—and I know that it will last and guide us long after I am gone.

When Roy Wilkins joined the NAACP in 1931, three blacks per month were lynched in the United States of America, and when Roy Wilkins left the NAACP, the Supreme Court ruled segregation unlawful. The Civil Rights Act, The Voting Act, and the Fair Housing Act were passed. Roy Wilkins and his NAACP family changed America. This was done with a faith and understanding of American society and the fighting spirit of Afro-Americans and their allies. The cost was dear: Wharlest Jackson, Medgar Evers, Vernon Dahmer, James Reeb, and so many others paid with their lives. The work, the sacrifice, and dedicated commitment nourished Roy Wilkins and his wife Aminda. It was Dr. Benjamin Hooks who described Roy Wilkins' vision and the man:

"He was modest, but proud. He was reasonable, but bold."

Appendix of Documents

Document 1: What to the Slave Is the Fourth of July?

In 1852, the ex-slave Frederick Douglass was asked to speak at a Fourth of July celebration in Rochester, New York. A thundering orator, Douglass used the occasion to deliver a scathing critique of America and the institute of slavery.

Fellow-citizens, pardon me, allow me to ask, why am I called upon to speak here today? What have I, or those I represent, to do with your national independence? Are the great principles of political freedom and of natural justice, embodied in that Declaration of Independence, extended to us? And am I, therefore, called upon to bring our humble offering to the national altar, and to confess the benefits and express devout gratitude for the blessings resulting from your independence to us?

Would to God, both for your sakes and ours, that an affirmative answer could be truthfully returned to these questions! Then would my task be light, and my burden easy and delightful. For who is there so cold, that a nation's sympathy could not warm him? Who so obdurate and dead to the claims of gratitude, that would not thankfully acknowledge such priceless benefits? Who so stolid and selfish, that would not give his voice to swell the hallelujahs of a nation's jubilee when the chains of servitude had been torn from his limbs? I am not that man. In a case like that, the dumb might eloquently speak, and the "lame man leap as an hart."

But such is not the state of the case. I say it with a sad sense of the disparity between us. I am not included within the pale of this glorious anniversary! Your high independence only reveals the immeasurable distance between us. The blessings in which you, this day, rejoice, are not enjoyed in common. The rich inheritance of justice, liberty, prosperity, and independence, bequeathed by your fathers, is shared by you, not by me. The sunlight that brought light and healing to you has brought stripes and death to me. This Fourth of July is yours, not mine. You may rejoice, I must mourn. To drag a man in fetters into the grand illuminated temple of liberty, and call upon him to join you in joyous anthems, were inhuman mockery and sacreligious irony. Do you mean, citizens, to mock me, by asking me to speak today? If so, there is a parallel to your conduct. And let me warn you that it is dangerous to copy the example of a nation whose crimes, towering up to heaven, were thrown down by the breath of the Almighty, burying that nation in irrevocable ruin! I can today take up the plaintive lament of a peeled and woe-smitten people! . . .

What, to the American slave, is your Fourth of July? I answer: a day that reveals to him, more than all other days in the year, the gross injustice and cruelty of which he is the constant victim. To him, your celebration is a sham; your boasted liberty, an unholy license; your national greatness, swelling vanity. Your sounds of rejoicing are empty and heartless; your denunciation of tyrants, brass-fronted impudence; your shouts of liberty and equality, hollow mockery; your prayers and hymns, your sermons and thanksgivings, with all your religious parade and solemnity, are, to him, mere bombast, fraud, deception, impiety, and hypocrisy—a thin veil to cover up crimes which would disgrace a nation of savages. There is not a nation on the earth guilty of practices more shocking and bloody than are the people of the United States, at this very hour.

Go where you may, search where you will, roam through all the monarchies and despotisms of the Old World, travel through South America, search out every abuse, and when you have found the last, lay your facts by the side of the everyday practices of this nation, and you will say with me that, for revolting barbarity and shameless hypocrisy, America reigns without a rival.

Frederick Douglass, speech delivered at Rochester, New York, July 5, 1852.

Document 2: The Atlanta Compromise

In 1895, Booker T. Washington delivered an address at the Cotton States and International Exposition in Atlanta, Georgia. The speech, excerpted here, contains the essence of Washington's racial philosophy—that vocational training and economic self-reliance were the best routes to social and political equality. It would become his most famous speech, although many black leaders, most notably W.E.B. Du Bois, objected to Washington's doctrine of accommodation.

A ship lost at sea for many days suddenly sighted a friendly vessel. From the mast of the unfortunate vessel was seen a signal, "Water, water; we die of thirst!" The answer from the friendly vessel at once came back, "Cast down your bucket where you are." A second time the signal, "Water, water; send us water!" ran up from the distressed vessel, and was answered, "Cast down your bucket where you are." And a third and fourth signal for water was answered, "Cast down your bucket where you are." The captain of the distressed vessel, at last heeding the injunction, cast down his bucket, and it came up full of fresh, sparkling water from the mouth of the Amazon River.

To those of my race who depend on bettering their condition in a foreign land or who underestimate the importance of cultivating friendly relations with the Southern white man, who is their next-door neighbor, I would say: "Cast down your bucket where you are"—cast it down in making friends in every manly way of the people of all races by whom we are surrounded.

Cast it down in agriculture, mechanics, in commerce, in domestic service, and in the professions. And in this connection it is well to bear in mind that whatever other sins the South may be called to bear, when it comes to business, pure and simple, it is in the South that the Negro is given a man's chance in the commercial world, and in nothing is this Exposition more eloquent than in emphasizing this chance. Our greatest danger is that in the great leap from slavery to freedom we may overlook the fact that the masses of us are to live by the productions of our hands, and fail to keep in mind that we shall prosper in proportion as we learn to dignify and glorify common labor, and put brains and skill into the common occupations of life; shall prosper in proportion as we learn to draw the line between the superficial and the substantial, the ornamental gewgaws of life and the useful. No race can prosper till it learns that there is as much dignity in tilling a field as in writing a poem. It is at the bottom of life we must begin, and not at the top. Nor should we permit our grievances to overshadow our opportunities.

To those of the white race who look to the incoming of those of foreign birth and strange tongue and habits for the prosperity of the South, were I permitted I would repeat what I say to my own race, "Cast down your bucket where you are." Cast it down among the eight millions of Negroes whose habits you know, whose fidelity and love you have tested in days when to have proved treacherous meant the ruin of your firesides. Cast down your bucket among these people who have, without strikes and labor wars, tilled your fields, cleared your forests, builded your railroads and cities, and brought forth treasures from the bowels of the earth, and helped make possible this magnificent representation of the progress of the South. Casting down your bucket among my people, helping and encouraging them as you are doing on these grounds, and to education of head, hand, and heart, you will find that they will buy your surplus land, make blossom the waste places in your fields, and run your factories. While doing this, you can be sure in the future, as in the past, that you and your families will be surrounded by the most patient, faithful, law-abiding, and unresentful people that the world has seen. As we have proved our loyalty to you in the past, in nursing your children, watching by the sickbed of your mothers and fathers, and often following them with tear-dimmed eyes to their graves, so in the future, in our humble way, we shall stand by you with a devotion that no foreigner can approach, ready to lay down our lives, if need be, in defense of yours, interlacing our industrial, commercial, civil, and religious life with yours in a way that shall make the interests of both races one. In all things that are purely social, we can be as separate as the fingers, yet one as the hand in all things essential to mutual progress.

There is no defense or security for any of us except in the

highest intelligence and development of all. If anywhere there are efforts tending to curtail the fullest growth of the Negro, let these efforts be turned into stimulating, encouraging, and making him the most useful and intelligent citizen. Effort or means so invested will pay a thousand percent interest. These efforts will be twice blessed—blessing him that gives and him that takes.

Booker T. Washington, speech at the Cotton States and International Exposition, Atlanta, Georgia, September 18, 1895.

Document 3: The Negro Problem

In The Souls of Black Folk, *published in 1903, W.E.B. Du Bois describes the black experience in America—and the impact of oppression—at the dawn of the twentieth century.*

Between me and the other world there is ever an unasked question: unasked by some through feelings of delicacy; by others through the difficulty of rightly framing it. All, nevertheless, flutter round it. They approach me in a half-hesitant sort of way, eye me curiously or compassionately, and then, instead of saying directly, How does it feel to be a problem? they say, I know an excellent colored man in my town; or, I fought at Mechanicsville; or, Do not these Southern outrages make your blood boil? At these I smile, or am interested, or reduce the boiling to a simmer, as the occasion may require. To the real question, How does it feel to be a problem? I answer seldom a word.

And yet, being a problem is a strange experience—peculiar even for one who has never been anything else, save perhaps in babyhood and in Europe. It is in the early days of rollicking boyhood that the revelation first bursts upon one, all in a day, as it were. I remember well when the shadow swept across me. I was a little thing, away up in the hills of New England, where the dark Housatonic winds between Hoosac and Taghkanic to the sea. In a wee wooden schoolhouse, something put it into the boys' and girls' heads to buy gorgeous visiting-cards—ten cents a package—and exchange. The exchange was merry, till one girl, a tall newcomer, refused my card,—refused it peremptorily, with a glance. Then it dawned upon me with a certain suddenness that I was different from the others; or like, mayhap, in heart and life and longing, but shut out from their world by a vast veil. I had thereafter no desire to tear down that veil, to creep through; I held all beyond it in common contempt, and lived above it in a region of blue sky and great wandering shadows. That sky was bluest when I could beat my mates at examination-time, or beat them at a foot-race, or even beat their stringy heads. Alas, with the years all this fine contempt began to fade; for the worlds I longed for, and all their dazzling opportunities, were theirs, not mine. But they should not keep these prizes, I said; some, all, I would wrest from them. Just how I would do it I could never decide: by reading law, by healing the sick, by telling the wonderful tales that swam in my head,—some way. With other black boys the strife was not so fiercely sunny: their youth shrunk into tasteless sycophancy, or into silent hatred of the pale world about them and mocking distrust of everything white; or wasted itself in a bitter cry, Why did God make me an outcast and a stranger in mine own house? The shades of the prison-house closed round about us all: walls strait and stubborn to the whitest, but relentlessly narrow, tall, and unscalable to sons of night who must plod darkly on in resignation, or beat unavailing palms against the stone, or steadily, half hopelessly, watch the streak of blue above.

After the Egyptian and Indian, the Greek and Roman, the Teuton and Mongolian, the Negro is a sort of seventh son, born with a veil, and gifted with second-sight in this American world,—a world which yields him no true self-consciousness, but only lets him see himself through the revelation of the other world. It is a peculiar sensation, this double-consciousness, this sense of always looking at one's self through the eyes of others, of measuring one's soul by the tape of a world that looks on in amused contempt and pity. One ever feels his twoness,—an American, a Negro; two souls, two thoughts, two unreconciled strivings; two warring ideals in one dark body, whose dogged strength alone keeps it from being torn asunder.

The history of the American Negro is the history of this

strife,—this longing to attain self-conscious manhood, to merge his double self into a better and truer self. In this merging he wishes neither of the older selves to be lost. He would not Africanize America, for America has too much to teach the world and Africa. He would not bleach his Negro soul in a flood of white Americanism, for he knows that Negro blood has a message for the world. He simply wishes to make it possible for a man to be both a Negro and an American, without being cursed and spit upon by his fellows, without having the doors of Opportunity closed roughly in his face.

W.E.B. Du Bois, *The Souls of Black Folk.* New York: Dodd, Mead, 1961.

Document 4: The Aims of the Universal Negro Improvement Association

In 1914, Marcus Garvey founded the Universal Negro Improvement Association (UNIA) to give expression to his political ideas and to promote the establishment of a separate black society. In its day, the UNIA was the most powerful organization of black people in the world.

Generally the public is kept misinformed of the truth surrounding new movements of reform. Very seldom, if ever, reformers get the truth told about them and their movements. Because of this natural attitude, the Universal Negro Improvement Association has been greatly handicapped in its work, causing thereby one of the most liberal and helpful human movements of the twentieth century to be held up to ridicule by those who take pride in poking fun at anything not already successfully established.

The white man of America has become the natural leader of the world. He, because of his exalted position, is called upon to help in all human efforts. From nations to individuals the appeal is made to him for aid in all things affecting humanity, so, naturally, there can be no great mass movement or change without first acquainting the leader on whose sympathy and advice the world moves.

It is because of this, and more so because of a desire to be Christian friends with the white race, why I explain the aims and objects of the Universal Negro Improvement Association.

The Universal Negro Improvement Association is an organization among Negroes that is seeking to improve the condition of the race, with the view of establishing a nation in Africa where Negroes will be given the opportunity to develop by themselves, without creating the hatred and animosity that now exist in countries of the white race through Negroes rivaling them for the highest and best positions in government, politics, society and industry. The organization believes in the rights of all men, yellow, white and black. To us, the white race has a right to the peaceful possession and occupation of countries of its own and in like manner the yellow and black races have their rights. It is only by an honest and liberal consideration of such rights can the world be blessed with the peace that is sought by Christian teachers and leaders.

Marcus Garvey, "Aims and Objects of Movement for Solution of Negro Problem," in Amy Jacques-Garvey, ed., *The Philosophy and Opinions of Marcus Garvey*. New York: Universal, 1925.

Document 5: The March on Washington Address

The preeminent labor leader of the early twentieth century, A. Philip Randolph sought to dismantle not only discrimination in the defense industries and unfair labor practices, but also black oppression in general. An eloquent speaker, Randolph set forth his ideology in an address, excerpted here, to a special conference of the 1941 March on Washington Movement, a precursor to the now famous 1963 March on Washington.

Thus our feet are set in the path toward [the long-range goal of] equality—economic, political and social and racial. Equality is the heart and essence of democracy, freedom and justice. Without equality of opportunity in industry, in labor unions, schools and colleges, government, politics and before the law, without equality in social relations and in all phases of human endeavor, the Negro is certain to be consigned to an inferior status. There must be no dual standards of justice, no dual rights, privileges, duties or responsibilities of citizenship. No dual forms of freedom. . . .

But our nearer goals include the abolition of discrimination, segregation, and Jim-Crow in the Government, the Army, Navy, Air Corps, U.S. Marines, Coast Guard, Women's Auxiliary Army Corps and the Waves, and defense industries; the elimination of discriminations in hotels, restaurants, on public transportation conveyances, in educational, recreational, cultural, and amusement and entertainment places such as theatres, beaches, and so forth.

We want the full works of citizenship with no reservations. We will accept nothing less.

But goals must be achieved. They are not secured because it is just and right that they be possessed by Negro or white people. Slavery was not abolished because it was bad and unjust. It was abolished because men fought, bled and died on the battlefield.

Therefore, if Negroes secure their goals, immediate and remote, they must win them and to win them they must fight, sacrifice, suffer, go to jail and, if need be, die for them. These rights will not be given. They must be taken.

Daniel J. O'Neill, ed., *Speeches by Black Americans.* Encino, CA: Dickenson, 1971.

Document 6: *Brown v. Board of Education*

In the landmark Brown v. Board of Education of Topeka, Kansas, *the Supreme Court reversed its 1896 ruling in* Plessy v. Ferguson, *the historic case that made "separate but equal" a legal doctrine. In the* Brown *decision, Chief Justice Earl Warren declared that segregated educational facilities were inherently unequal and therefore unconstitutional.*

Today, education is perhaps the most important function of state and local governments. Compulsory school attendance laws and the great expenditures for education both demonstrate our recognition of the importance of education to our democratic society. It is required in the performance of our most basic public responsibilities, even service in the armed forces. It is the very foundation of good citizenship. Today it is a principal instrument in awakening the child to cultural values, in preparing him for later professional training, and in helping him to adjust normally to his environment. In these days, it is doubtful that any child may reasonably be expected to succeed in life if he is denied the opportunity of an education. Such an opportunity, where the state has undertaken to provide it, is a right which must be made available to all on equal terms.

We come then to the question presented: Does segregation of children in public schools solely on the basis of race, even though the physical facilities and other "tangible" factors may be equal, deprive the children of the minority group of equal educational opportunities? We believe that it does.

In *Sweatt v. Painter, supra*, in finding that a segregated law school for Negroes could not provide them equal educational opportunities, this Court relied in large part on "those qualities which are incapable of objective measurement but which make for greatness in a law school." In *McLaurin v. Oklahoma State Regents, supra*, the Court, in requiring that a Negro admitted to a white graduate school be treated like all other students, again resorted to intangible considerations: ". . . his ability to study, to engage in discussions and exchange views with other students, and, in general, to learn his profession." Such considerations apply with added force to children in grade and high schools. To separate them from others of similar age and qualifications solely because of their race generates a feeling of inferiority as to their status in the community that may affect their hearts and minds in a way unlikely ever to be undone. The effect of this separation on their educational opportunities was well stated by a finding in the Kansas case by a court which nevertheless felt compelled to rule against the Negro plaintiffs:

Segregation of white and colored children in public schools has a detrimental effect upon the colored children. The impact is greater when it has the sanction of the law, for the policy of separating the races is usually interpreted as denoting the inferiority of the negro group. A sense of inferiority affects the motivation of a child to learn. Segregation with the sanction of law, therefore, has a tendency to [retard] the educational and mental development of negro children and to deprive them of some of the benefits they would receive in a racial[ly] integrated school system.

Whatever may have been the extent of psychological knowledge at the time of *Plessy v. Ferguson*, this finding is amply supported by modern authority. Any language in *Plessy v. Ferguson* contrary to this finding is rejected.

We conclude that, in the field of public education, the doctrine of "separate but equal" has no place. Separate educational facilities are inherently unequal. Therefore, we hold that the plaintiffs and others similarly situated for whom the actions have been brought are, by reason of the segregation complained of, deprived of the equal protection of the laws guaranteed by the Fourteenth Amendment. This disposition makes unnecessary any discussion whether such segregation also violates the Due Process Clause of the Fourteenth Amendment.

Earl Warren, *Brown v. Board of Education of Topeka, Kansas*, 349 U.S. 294, 1955. From the Legal Information Institute, Cornell Law Library, www.law.cornell.edu.

Document 7: The Right of Protest

As chief counsel of the National Association for the Advancement of Colored People (NAACP), Thurgood Marshall took on many legal battles to further civil rights. In the following excerpt from an address at a 1960 NAACP meeting, the tenacious lawyer explains why he upholds—and will staunchly defend—the right of protest as a democratic means of advancing black causes.

While the cry is against apartheid in South Africa, is for one man, one vote in Kenya, is for the right to register and vote in Mississippi and Alabama, the right to non-discriminatory service in stores throughout the South, the right to non-segregated education in the South or the ending of subtle segregation in the North, the cry for freedom is increasing in tempo throughout the world. Thus, the sit-in strikes of young people throughout the South is the latest evidence of this wave. We believe that those of us in the NAACP and other organizations who have fought so long in this fight must continue the type of leadership that brings about the lawful and orderly step by step march toward freedom from racial discrimination wherever it exists.

One writer, in commenting upon the situation in sit-in strikes says: "It seems rather ridiculous when you can buy a nice hat for eight or ten dollars in the store and yet you can't satisfy, without discrimination, the very fundamental need of your own hunger with a cup of coffee and a sandwich."

Thus young people, in the true tradition of our democratic principles, are fighting the matter for all of us and they are doing it in a most effective way. Protest—the right of protest—is basic to a democratic form of government. The right of petition; the right of assembly; the right of freedom of speech are so basic to our government that they are enshrined in the very first amendment to the Constitution. And the 14th Amendment says that no state shall throttle these freedoms.

These young people are just simply sick and tired of waiting patiently without protest for the rights they know to be theirs. Consequently, they settled upon the right of peaceful protests—and what is wrong with that?

As a result of these peaceful protests, the whole force of state government has been arrayed behind the private store owner to prevent peaceful protests. The students have been arrested on every possible type of criminal charge.

In some areas they are charged with trespassing because they refuse to leave the establishment; because they came on the property when told not to do so, or are charged with having threatened some one. Secondly, many of them have been charged with violation of fire department regulations such as blocking of aisles of a store despite the fact that no one has ever been charged with the same crime before;

Thirdly, some are charged with assault for refusing to move or allegedly brushing against someone;

Fourth, some are charged with failure to obtain licenses for public meetings or parades; and

Fifth, authorities have dragged out the old disorderly conduct procedure.

There will be many others thought up by lawyers well-paid and well trained in the law. And here we have once again the example of the full strength of a state government, paid for by white and black taxes, arrayed against young people solely because of their race and color.

In Orangeburg, South Carolina, 450 students were arrested walking down the street before they had even started to picket or to parade and everyone is to be tried in blocs of fifteen per day. This is obviously done in the hope of wearing our legal staff and our pocketbook down. We have news for them. We are prepared to stay in court after court, in city after city and in state after state as long as they can stay there.

On Thursday, March 17, in Little Rock, Arkansas, fifteen students peacefully protesting were seized and fined $250, and sentenced to thirty days in jail.

Each of these instances can be cited in state after state wherever the protests have been made. To all of this, we have but one reply, even one word and the word is SHAME.

Whenever you read about it—

Whenever you hear about it—

Whenever you hear it discussed—say SHAME—SHAME on those who under the guise of states' rights or state law seek to throttle young people lawfully protesting.

Say SHAME on the white people of the South, the good white people, the so-called moderates who sit idly by and allow young people to be persecuted solely because of their race or color. And when you hear a Negro who has been adequately brainwashed say that this is too much to do just to get a hamburger or a frankfurter, to him say SHAME. For this that the young people are doing is for the best interest of all of us and indeed for the country itself.

We have just completed a lawyers conference in Washington attended by lawyers handling the sit-in cases from Delaware to the Gulf of Mexico. We have compared notes. We have shared our legal thoughts, our legal briefs and legal procedures. We are as a unit. We are going to work in the most cooperative fashion. We are going to give to these young people the best legal defense available to them. Negroes and other Americans who believe in freedom will provide the bail money for them. Once again we are called upon to use our private resources, our private strength, and our private abilities to save the good name of this country.

Roy L. Hill, *Rhetoric of Racial Revolt.* Denver, CO: Golden Bell Press, 1964.

Document 8: Separation or Integration?

James Farmer was one of the founders of the Congress of Racial Equality (CORE), an interracial civil rights organization that pioneered nonviolent direct action as a weapon against segregation and other forms of discrimination. In 1962, Farmer—a committed integrationist—was asked to debate Malcolm X, whose militant views ran counter to his own. The following is a portion of Farmer's rebuttal to the Muslim leader and his separatist credo.

I think that Mr. X's views are utterly impractical and that his so-called "black state" cannot be achieved. There is no chance of getting it unless it is to be given to us by Allah. We have waited for a long time for God to give us other things and we have found that the God in which most of us happen to believe helps those who help themselves. So we would like you to tell us, Mr. X, just what steps you plan to go through to get this black state. Is it one that is going to be gotten by violence, by force? Is it going to be given to us by the Federal government? Once a state is allocated, then are the white people who happen to live there to be moved out forcibly, or Negroes who don't want to go to your black state going to be moved in forcibly? And what does this do to their liberty and freedom?

Now Mr. X suggests that we Negroes or so-called Negroes, as he puts it, ought to go back where we came from. You know, this is a very interesting idea. I think the solution to many of the problems, including the economic problem of our country, would be for all of us to go back where we came from and leave the country to the American Indians. As a matter of fact, maybe the American Indian can go back to Asia, where I understand the anthropologists tell us he came from, and I don't know who preceded him there. But if we search back far enough I am sure that we can find some people to people or populate this nation. Now the overwhelming number of Negroes in this country consider it to be their country; their country more than Africa: I was in Africa three years ago, and while I admire and respect what is being done there, while there is certainly a definite sense of identification, and sympathy with what is going on there, the fact is that the cultures are so very different. Mr. X, I am sure that you have much more in common with me or with several people whom I see sitting here than you do with the Africans, than you do with Tom Mboya. Most of them could not understand you, or you they, because they speak Swahili or some other language and you would have to learn those languages.

I tell you that we are Americans. This is our country as much as it is white American. Negroes came as slaves, most of us did. Many white people came as indentured servants, indentured servants are not free. Don't forget it wasn't all of you who were on that ship, The Mayflower.

Now separation of course has been proposed as the answer to the problem, rather than integration. I am pleased however that Malcolm, oh pardon me, Mr. X, indicated that if integration works, and if it provides dignity, then we are for integration. Apparently he is almost agreeing with us there. He is sort of saying as King Agrippa said to St. Paul, "Almost Thou Persuadest Me." I hope that he will be able to come forth and make the additional step and join me at the integrationist side of this table. In saying that separation really is the answer and the most effective solution to this problem, he draws a distinction between separation and segregation, saying that segregation is forced ghettoism while separation is voluntary ghettoism. Well now, I would like to ask Mr. X whether it would be voluntary for Negroes to be segregated as long as we allow discrimination in housing throughout our country to exist. If you live in a black state and cannot get a house elsewhere, then are you voluntarily separated, or are you forcibly segregated?

James Farmer, debate at Cornell University, March 7, 1962. From Francis L. Broderick and August Meier, *Negro Protest Thought in the Twentieth Century*. New York: Bobbs-Merrill, 1965.

Document 9: Letter from Birmingham Jail

In the spring of 1963, Martin Luther King Jr. and other civil rights leaders staged a large-scale series of sit-ins, marches, pickets, and boycotts in a campaign to desegregate Birmingham. These protests ignited a violent reaction: Ardent segregationists attempted to disperse crowds by turning police dogs and fire hoses on the non-violent demonstrators. Hundreds of protesters were arrested. While incarcerated, King composed a now-famous letter to a group of Alabama clergymen who had criticized his activities in Birmingham.

You may well ask: "Why direct action? Why sit-ins, marches and so forth? Isn't negotiation a better path?" You are quite right in calling, for negotiation. Indeed, this is the very purpose of direct action. Nonviolent direct action seeks to create such a crisis and foster such a tension that a community which has constantly refused to negotiate is forced to confront the issue. It seeks so to dramatize the issue that it can no longer be ignored. My citing the creation of tension as part of the work of the nonviolent-resister may sound rather shocking. But I must confess that I am not afraid of the word "tension." I have earnestly opposed violent tension, but there is a type of constructive, nonviolent tension which is necessary for growth. Just as Socrates felt that it was necessary to create a tension in the mind so that individuals could rise from the bondage of myths and half-truths to the unfettered realm of creative analysis and objective appraisal, we must see the need for nonviolent gadflies to create the kind of tension in society that will help men rise from the dark depths of prejudice and racism to the majestic heights of understanding and brotherhood.

The purpose of our direct-action program is to create a situation so crisis-packed that it will inevitably open the door to negotiation. I therefore concur with you in your call for negotiation. Too long has our beloved Southland been bogged down in a tragic effort to live in monologue rather than dialogue. . . .

We know through painful experience that freedom is never voluntarily given by the oppressor; it must be demanded by the oppressed. Frankly, I have yet to engage in a direct-action campaign that was "well timed" in the view of those who have not suffered unduly from the disease of segregation. For years now I have heard the word "Wait!" It rings in the ear of every Negro with piercing familiarity. This "Wait" has almost always meant "Never." We must come to see, with one of our distinguished jurists, that "justice too long delayed is justice denied."

We have waited for more than 340 years for our constitutional and God-given rights. The nations of Asia and Africa are moving with jetlike speed toward gaining political independence, but we still creep at horse-and-buggy pace toward gaining a cup of coffee at a lunch counter. Perhaps it is easy for those who have never felt the stinging darts of segregation to say, "Wait." But when you have seen vicious mobs lynch your mothers and fathers at will and drown your sisters and brothers at whim; when you have seen hate-filled policemen curse, kick and even kill your black brothers and sisters; when you see the vast majority of your twenty million Negro brothers smothering in an airtight cage of poverty in the midst of an affluent society; when you suddenly find your tongue twisted and your speech stammering as you seek to explain to your six-year-old daughter why she can't go to the public amusement park that has just been advertised on television, and see tears welling up in her eyes when she is told that Funtown is closed to colored children, and see ominous clouds of inferiority beginning to form in her little mental sky, and see her beginning to distort her personality by developing an unconscious bitterness toward white people; when you have to concoct an answer for a five-year-old son who is asking: "Daddy, why do white people treat colored people so mean?"; when you take a cross-county drive and find it necessary to sleep night after night in the uncomfortable corners of your automobile because no motel will accept you; when you are humiliated day in and day out by nagging signs reading "white" and "colored"; when your first name becomes "nigger," your middle name becomes "boy" (however old you are) and your last name becomes "John," and your wife and mother are never given the respected title "Mrs."; when you are harried by day and haunted by night by the fact that you are a Negro, living constantly at tiptoe stance, never quite knowing what to expect next, and are plagued with inner fears and outer resentments; when you are forever fighting a degenerating sense of "nobodiness" then you will understand why we find it difficult to wait. There comes a time when the cup of endurance runs over, and men are no longer willing to be plunged into the abyss of despair. I hope, sirs, you can understand our legitimate and unavoidable impatience.

Martin Luther King Jr., "Letter from Birmingham Jail," www.nobelprizes.com.

Document 10: John Lewis at the March on Washington

A vocal opponent of federal civil rights legislation, which he deemed inadequate, John Lewis exhorted blacks to use bold action campaigns to combat racism. At the 1963 March on Washington, Lewis, then chairman of the Student Nonviolent Coordinating Committee (SNCC), planned to express his views in the following speech. At the request of other civil rights leaders, Lewis softened the radical tone of the speech prior to the march.

We march today for jobs and freedom, but we have nothing to be proud of, for hundreds and thousands of our brothers are not here—for they have no money for their transportation, for they are receiving starvation wages . . . or no wages at all.

In good conscience, we cannot support the administration's civil-rights bill, for it is too little, and too late. There's not one thing in the bill that will protect our people from police brutality.

The voting section of this bill will not help the thousands of citizens who want to vote; will not help the citizens of Mississippi, of Alabama and Georgia who are qualified to vote, who are without a sixth-grade education. "One Man, One Vote," is the African cry. It is ours, too.

People have been forced to move for they have exercised their right to register to vote. What is in the bill that will protect the homeless and starving people of this nation? What is there in this bill to insure the equality of a maid who earns five dollars a week in the home of a family whose income is a hundred thousand dollars a year?

This bill will not protect young children and old women from police dogs and fire hoses for engaging in peaceful demonstrations. This bill will not protect the citizens in Danville, Virginia, who must live in constant fear in a police state. This bill will not protect the hundreds of people who have been arrested on trumped-up charges, like those in Americus, Georgia, where four young men are in jail, facing a death penalty, for engaging in peaceful protest.

For the first time in a hundred years this nation is being awakened to the fact that segregation is evil and it must be destroyed in all forms. Our presence today proves that we have been aroused to the point of action.

We are now involved in a serious revolution. This nation is still a place of cheap political leaders allying themselves with open forms of political, economic and social exploitation.

In some parts of the South we have worked in the fields from sun-up to sun-down for twelve dollars a week. In Albany, Georgia, we have seen our people indicted by the federal government for peaceful protest, while the Deputy Sheriff beat Attorney C.B. King and left him half-dead; while local police officials kicked and assaulted the pregnant wife of Slater King, and she lost her baby.

It seems to me that the Albany indictment is part of a conspiracy on the part of the federal government and local politicians for political expediency.

I want to know, Which side is the federal government on?

The revolution is at hand, and we must free ourselves of the chains of political and economic slavery. The nonviolent revolution is saying, "We will not wait for the courts to act, for we have been waiting hundreds of years. We will not wait for the President, nor the Justice Department, nor Congress, but we will take matters into our own hands, and create a great source of power, outside of any national structure that could and would assure us victory." For those who have said, "Be patient and wait!" we must say, "Patience is a dirty and nasty word." We cannot be patient, we do not want to be free gradually, we want our freedom, and we want it now.

Philip S. Foner, *The Voice of Black America*. New York: Simon and Schuster, 1972.

Document 11: The Black Revolution

In a 1964 speech in New York, Malcolm X condemned compla-
cency in the white community and issued the following warning:
Although indeed a minority group, black nationalists and Muslims
could ignite a revolutionary movement that would unite the entire
black community.

There are whites in this country who are still complacent
when they see the possibilities of racial strife getting out of
hand. You are complacent simply because you think you outnumber the racial minority in this country; what you have to
bear in mind is wherein you might outnumber us in this
country, you don't outnumber us all over the earth.

Any kind of racial explosion that takes place in this country today, in 1964, is not a racial explosion that can be confined to the shores of America. It is a racial explosion that
can ignite the racial powder keg that exists all over the planet
that we call earth. I think that nobody would disagree that
the dark masses of Africa and Asia and Latin America are already seething with bitterness, animosity, hostility, unrest,
and impatience with the racial intolerance that they themselves have experienced at the hands of the white West.

And just as they have the ingredients of hostility toward
the West in general, here we also have 22 million African-
Americans, black, brown, red, and yellow people, in this
country who are also seething with bitterness and impatience
and hostility and animosity at the racial intolerance not only
of the white West but of white America in particular.

And by the hundreds of thousands today we find our own
people have become impatient, turning away from your
white nationalism, which you call democracy, toward the
militant, uncompromising policy of black nationalism. I
point out right here that as soon as we announced we were
going to start a black nationalist party in this country, we received mail from coast to coast, especially from young
people at the college level, the university level, who expressed complete sympathy and support and a desire to take
an active part in any kind of political action based on black
nationalism, designed to correct or eliminate immediately

evils that our people have suffered here for 400 years.

The black nationalists to many of you may represent only a minority in the community. And therefore you might have a tendency to classify them as something insignificant. But just as the fuse is the smallest part or the smallest piece in the powder keg, it is yet that little fuse that ignites the entire powder keg. The black nationalists to you may represent a small minority in the so-called Negro community. But they just happen to be composed of the type of ingredient necessary to fuse or ignite the entire black community.

And this is one thing that whites—whether you call yourselves liberals or conservatives or racists or whatever else you might choose to be—one thing that you have to realize is, where the black community is concerned, although the large majority you come in contact with may impress you as being moderate and patient and loving and long-suffering and all that kind of stuff, the minority who you consider to be Muslims or nationalists happen to be made of the type of ingredient that can easily spark the black community. This should be understood. Because to me a powder keg is nothing without a fuse.

1964 will be America's hottest year; her hottest year yet; a year of much racial violence and much racial bloodshed. But it won't be blood that's going to flow only on one side. The new generation of black people that have grown up in this country during recent years are already forming the opinion, and it's a just opinion, that if there is to be bleeding, it should be reciprocal—bleeding on both sides.

George Breitman, ed., *Malcolm X Speaks*. New York: Grove Weidenfeld, 1965.

Document 12: The Incorrigible Fannie Lou Hamer

With her harrowing personal accounts of Jim Crow, Fannie Lou Hamer became one of the civil rights movement's most effective spokespersons. She is perhaps best remembered for her widely publicized testimony of the hardships she encountered as she sought to exercise her constitutional voting rights.

I married in 1944 and stayed on the plantation until 1962

when I went down to the courthouse in Indianola to register to vote. That happened because I went to a mass meeting one night.

Until then I'd never heard of no mass meeting and I didn't know that a Negro could register and vote. Bob Moses, Reggie Robinson, Jim Bevel and James Forman were some of the SNCC workers who ran that meeting. When they asked for those to raise their hands who'd go down to the court-house the next day, I raised mine. Had it up as high as I could get it. I guess if I'd had any sense I'd a-been a little scared, but what was the point of being scared? The only thing they could do to me was kill me and it seemed like they'd been trying to do that a little bit at a time ever since I could re-member. Well, there was eighteen of us who went down to the courthouse that day and all of us were arrested. Police said the bus was painted the wrong color—said it was too yellow. After I got bailed out I went back to the plantation where Pap and I had lived for eighteen years. My oldest girl met me and told me that Mr. Marlow, the plantation owner, was mad and raising sand. He had heard that I had tried to register. That night he called on us and said, "We're not go-ing to have this in Mississippi and you will have to withdraw. I am looking for your answer, yea or nay?" I just looked. He said, "I will give you until tomorrow morning. And if you don't withdraw you will have to leave. If you do go withdraw, it's only how I feel, you might still have to leave." So I left that same night. Pap had to stay on till work on the planta-tion was through. Ten days later they fired into Mrs. Tucker's house where I was staying. They also shot two girls at Mr. Sissel's.

That was a rough winter. I hadn't a chance to do any can-ning before I got kicked off, so didn't have hardly anything. I always can more than my family can use 'cause there's always people who don't have enough. That winter was bad, though. Pap couldn't get a job nowhere 'cause everybody knew he was my husband. We made it on through, though, and since then I just been trying to work and get our people organized.

I reckon the most horrible experience I've had was in June of 1963. I was arrested along with several others in Winona,

Mississippi. That's in Montgomery County, the county where I was born. I was carried to a cell and locked up with Euvester Simpson. I began to hear the sound of licks, and I could hear people screaming. . . .

After then, the State Highway patrolmen came and carried me out of the cell into another cell where there were two Negro prisoners. The patrolman gave the first Negro a long blackjack that was heavy. It was loaded with something and they had me lay down on the bunk with my face down, and I was beat. I was beat by the first Negro till he gave out. Then the patrolman ordered the other man to take the blackjack and he began to beat.

Fannie Lou Hamer, *To Praise Our Bridges: An Autobiography.* Jackson, MS: KIPCO, 1967.

Chronology

1619
The first African slaves are brought to North America.

1863
President Abraham Lincoln issues the Emancipation Proclamation.

1865
The Reconstruction era begins; the Thirteenth Amendment abolishes slavery in the United States.

1866
The Civil Rights Act of 1866 grants blacks U.S. citizenship; the Fourteenth Amendment reaffirms citizenship rights for blacks and gives all citizens full and equal protection under the law.

1870
The Fifteenth Amendment grants black males the right to vote.

1875
The Civil Rights Act of 1875 guarantees black Americans equal access to public facilities.

1876
Reconstruction ends.

1881
Booker T. Washington founds the Tuskegee Institute, a vocational school for blacks.

1883
The Supreme Court overturns the Civil Rights Act of 1875.

1890
The state of Mississippi adopts poll taxes and literacy tests to disfranchise black voters.

1895
Booker T. Washington delivers his Atlanta Exposition speech, which accepts segregation of the races.

1896
The Supreme Court rules in *Plessy v. Ferguson* that separate but equal treatment of the races is constitutional.

1900–1915
Over one thousand blacks are lynched in the states of the former Confederacy.

1905
The Niagara Movement is founded by W.E.B. Du Bois and other black leaders to urge more direct action to achieve black civil rights.

1909
The National Association for the Advancement of Colored People (NAACP) is organized.

1910
The National Urban League is founded to help the conditions of urban African Americans.

1925
Black nationalist leader Marcus Garvey is convicted of mail fraud.

1928
For the first time in the twentieth century an African American is elected to Congress.

1931
Farrad Muhammad establishes in Detroit what will become the Black Muslim Movement.

1933
The NAACP files—and loses—its first suit against segregation and discrimination in education.

1938
The Supreme Court orders the admission of a black applicant to the University of Missouri Law School.

1941
A. Philip Randolph threatens a massive march on Washington unless the Roosevelt administration takes measures to ensure black employment in defense industries; Roosevelt agrees to establish the Fair Employment Practices Committee (FEPC).

1942
The Congress of Racial Equality (CORE) is organized in Chicago.

1943
Race riots in Detroit and Harlem cause black leaders to ask their followers to be less demanding in asserting their commitment to civil rights; A. Philip Randolph breaks ranks to call for civil disobedience against Jim Crow schools and railroads.

1946
The Supreme Court, in *Morgan v. the Commonwealth of Virginia*, rules that state laws requiring racial segregation on buses violate the Constitution when applied to interstate passengers.

April 1947
Jackie Robinson breaks the color line in major league baseball.

April 9–23, 1947
Bayard Rustin organizes integrated group trips on trains and buses through Kentucky, Tennessee, North Carolina, and Virginia.

October 29, 1947
To Secure These Rights, the report by the President's Committee on Civil Rights, is released; the commission, appointed by President Harry S. Truman, calls for the elimination of racial segregation and recommends government action to secure civil rights for all Americans.

July 26, 1948
President Harry S. Truman issues an executive order desegregating the armed services.

June 1950
The NAACP decides to make its legal strategy a full-scale attack on educational segregation.

May 17, 1954
In *Brown v. Board of Education* the Supreme Court declares separate educational facilities "inherently unequal."

July 11, 1954
The First White Citizens Council meeting is held in Mississippi.

September 1954
The school year begins with the integration of 150 formerly segregated school districts in eight states; many other school districts remain segregated.

May 31, 1955
The Supreme Court, rejecting the NAACP's plea for com-

plete and total desegregation by September 1955, orders desegregation "with all deliberate speed."

September 23, 1955
An all-white jury finds defendants innocent of murdering black teenager Emmett Till after a nationally publicized trial; the defendants later confess to the killing.

November 1955
The Interstate Commerce Commission (ICC) bans racial segregation in all facilities and vehicles engaged in interstate transportation.

December 1, 1955
Rosa Parks is arrested for refusing to give up her bus seat to a white person; the action triggers a bus boycott in Montgomery, Alabama, led by Martin Luther King Jr.

January 30, 1956
The home of Martin Luther King Jr. is bombed.

February 3, 1956
Autherine Lucy wins a federal court order admitting her to the University of Alabama only to have the university permanently "expel" her; the University of Alabama remains segregated for seven more years.

March 12, 1956
One hundred one members of Congress from the South sign the "Southern Manifesto," decrying the *Brown v. Board of Education* decision.

June 1, 1956
Alabama outlaws the NAACP.

December 21, 1956
The Montgomery bus boycott ends after the city receives U.S. Supreme Court order to desegregate city buses.

January 11, 1957
Martin Luther King Jr. and a number of southern black clergymen create the Southern Christian Leadership Conference (SCLC).

August 29, 1957
Congress passes the first civil rights legislation since Reconstruction: The Civil Rights Act of 1957 establishes a civil rights division at the Justice Department and provides penalties for violating the voting rights of a U.S. citizen.

September 4, 1957
On the orders of Arkansas governor Orval Faubus, Arkansas National Guardsmen block nine black students from entering Central High School in Little Rock.

September 24, 1957
President Dwight D. Eisenhower dispatches one thousand paratroopers of the 101st Airborne Division to Little Rock to enforce a federal court order integrating Central High School.

September 29, 1958
The Supreme Court, in *Cooper v. Aaron*, rules that "evasive schemes" cannot be used to circumvent school desegregation.

October 25, 1958
Ten thousand students hold a Youth March for Integrated Schools in Washington, D.C.

1959
Sit-in campaigns by college students desegregate eating facilities in St. Louis, Chicago, and Bloomington, Indiana; the Tennessee Christian Leadership Conference holds brief sit-ins in Nashville department stores.

February 1, 1960
Four black students stage a sit-in at a Woolworth's lunch counter in Greensboro, North Carolina; the sit-in movement

to desegregate southern restaurants, hotels, movie theaters, libraries, and parks spreads to other southern states.

April 1960
The Student Nonviolent Coordinating Committee (SNCC) is formed at a student conference in Raleigh, North Carolina.

April 19, 1960
Twenty-five hundred students and community members in Nashville, Tennessee, stage a march on city hall—the first major demonstration of the civil rights movement—following the bombing of the home of a black lawyer.

May 6, 1960
President Eisenhower signs civil rights legislation authorizing federal judges to appoint referees to assist blacks seeking to register and to vote.

June 30, 1960
Zaire becomes the first of eleven African countries to gain independence within one year, inspiring many American blacks.

October 19, 1960
Martin Luther King Jr. is arrested during an Atlanta sit-in; Democratic presidential candidate John F. Kennedy telephones Mrs. King to express concern.

November 8, 1960
John F. Kennedy is elected president by a narrow margin.

December 5, 1960
The Supreme Court rules that discrimination in bus terminal restaurants is a violation of the Interstate Commerce Act.

March 13, 1961
James Farmer, national director of CORE, calls for volunteers to conduct "Freedom Rides" throughout the South.

Spring 1961
Martin Luther King Jr. and President John F. Kennedy hold a secret meeting at which King learns that the new president will not push hard for new civil rights legislation.

May 1961
White and black Freedom Riders are arrested and assaulted in North and South Carolina and Alabama; one bus is burned by a white mob; the CORE-sponsored Freedom Ride disbands and the movement is taken over by SNCC volunteers; the Kennedy administration sends federal marshals to assure the safety of the Freedom Riders.

June 16, 1961
U.S. attorney general Robert Kennedy meets with civil rights leaders and urges them to forgo demonstrations and Freedom Rides and to concentrate on winning the right to vote.

November 1961
Local black organizations in Albany, Georgia, form the Albany Movement to demonstrate for voting rights and desegregation.

December 1961
The SCLC meets with AFL-CIO leaders to strengthen ties between the two organizations.

December 11–14, 1961
Hundreds of demonstrators participate in marches in Albany, Georgia; Martin Luther King Jr. and aides arrive on December 15.

January 1962
FBI director J. Edgar Hoover writes Attorney General Robert Kennedy concerning Martin Luther King Jr.'s alleged ties to the Communist Party.

May 31, 1962
James Meredith files suit claiming racial discrimination after he is denied admission to the University of Mississippi.

August 1962
Albany Movement ends with many of its goals unmet.

August 7, 1962
A SNCC Voter Registration School opens in Pike County, Mississippi, marking the first such effort in the history of the state.

September 1962
Ku Klux Klan dynamite blasts destroy four black churches in Georgia towns.

September 30, 1962
President Kennedy federalizes the National Guard and sends several hundred federal marshals to Mississippi to guarantee James Meredith's admission to the University of Mississippi Law School over the opposition of Governor Ross Barnett and other whites; two persons are killed in a campus riot.

November 20, 1962
President Kennedy signs an executive order barring racial discrimination in federally financed housing.

February 2, 1963
Martin Luther King Jr. and other SCLC leaders arrive in Birmingham, Alabama, to lead a civil rights campaign; Robert Kennedy labels the effort "ill-timed" and urges King to abandon it.

Spring 1963
CORE takes the lead in protesting discrimination in northern cities.

April 1963
Martin Luther King Jr. opens his campaign to desegregate

Birmingham and is arrested on April 12; while incarcerated, King composes his "Letter from Birmingham City Jail."

May 3, 1963
Birmingham police chief Eugene "Bull" Connor turns police dogs and fire hoses against nonviolent demonstrators in Birmingham.

May 5, 1963
Three thousand protesters are jailed in Birmingham—the largest number of people imprisoned at any one time in the history of the civil rights movement.

May 10, 1963
An accord is reached in Birmingham; within ninety days lunch counters, restrooms, and drinking fountains will be desegregated in the city.

June 11, 1963
Black students Vivian Malone and James Hood enter the University of Alabama despite a demonstration of resistance by Governor George Wallace; in a nationally televised speech President John F. Kennedy calls segregation morally wrong.

June 12, 1963
NAACP field secretary Medgar Evers is shot and killed as he enters his home in Jackson, Mississippi.

June 19, 1963
Leaders of nearly one hundred corporations meet in New York City to pledge financial support for the civil rights movement.

July 18–23, 1963
Riots in Harlem follow the shooting of a fifteen-year-old black youth by an off-duty police officer.

August 28, 1963
Over 250,000 Americans gather at the Lincoln Memorial to

urge the passage of civil rights legislation and hear Martin Luther King Jr. deliver his "I Have a Dream" speech; Malcolm X dismisses the march as "the Farce on Washington."

September 15, 1963
Four young girls are killed when a bomb explodes at a Baptist church in Birmingham, Alabama.

October 10, 1963
Attorney General Robert Kennedy authorizes the wiretapping of Martin Luther King Jr.'s home phone in Atlanta.

November 22, 1963
President John F. Kennedy is assassinated; Vice President Lyndon B. Johnson assumes the presidency.

January 8, 1964
President Lyndon B. Johnson calls for passage of a civil rights act in his State of the Union address.

April 26, 1964
SNCC workers organize the Mississippi Freedom Democratic Party (MFDP).

Summer 1964
Enlisting the help of white volunteers, SNCC and CORE seek to register black voters across the South in the "Freedom Summer" campaign.

June 21, 1964
Three civil rights workers, Michael Schwerner and Andrew Goodman, both white New Yorkers, and James Chaney, a black student from Meridian, Mississippi, are murdered near Philadelphia, Mississippi.

July 2, 1964
President Lyndon B. Johnson signs the Civil Rights Act of 1964, which prohibits discrimination in most public accommodations, authorizes the federal government to withhold

funds from programs practicing discrimination, and creates the Equal Employment Opportunity Commission.

July 29, 1964
Several national civil rights leaders call for a moratorium on mass marches and demonstrations until after the November 3 presidential election.

August 22–26, 1964
At the Democratic National Convention in Atlantic City, New Jersey, delegates of the Mississippi Freedom Democratic Party ask to be seated as the legitimate Democratic Party of Mississippi; they refuse the compromise offer of two delegate seats.

September 14, 1964
New York City begins a program to end segregation by busing students.

November 3, 1964
Lyndon B. Johnson, with heavy black support, wins the presidential election by a wide margin over Barry Goldwater.

December 10, 1964
Martin Luther King Jr. is awarded the Nobel Peace Prize.

February 18, 1965
Civil rights marcher Jimmie Lee Jackson is shot and killed in Marion, Alabama.

February 21, 1965
Malcolm X is assassinated while addressing a rally of his followers in New York City; three black men are ultimately convicted of the murder.

March 7, 1965
"Bloody Sunday": Six hundred marchers outside Selma, Alabama, are attacked by state troopers with nightsticks and tear gas.

March 9, 1965
Martin Luther King Jr. leads a voting rights march in Selma but turns back before a state trooper barricade.

March 11, 1965
The death of white Unitarian minister James J. Reeb following a beating by local whites in Selma triggers demonstrations in many northern cities.

March 15, 1965
President Johnson delivers a televised speech to a joint session of Congress to request passage of a voting rights act.

March 21–25, 1965
Following a federal judge's court order allowing the march, and under federalized protection, Martin Luther King Jr. leads a voting rights march from Selma to Montgomery, Alabama.

August 6, 1965
President Johnson signs the Voting Rights Act of 1965, which outlaws literacy tests and empowers the Justice Department to supervise federal elections in seven southern states.

August 11–16, 1965
Rioting in the black ghetto of Watts in Los Angeles leads to thirty-five deaths, nine hundred injuries, and over thirty-five hundred arrests.

January 1966
Martin Luther King Jr. moves to Chicago to begin his first civil rights campaign in a northern city.

March 25, 1966
The Supreme Court bans poll taxes for all elections.

May 16, 1966
Stokely Carmichael replaces John Lewis as chairman of SNCC.

June 6, 1966
James Meredith is shot by a sniper while on a one-man "march against fear" in Mississippi.

June 7–26, 1966
Other civil rights leaders, including King and Carmichael, complete the "Meredith march"; the slogan "black power" is first used by Carmichael.

July 1966
The CORE national convention adopts a resolution in support of black power; the NAACP convention officially opposes the doctrine.

August 5, 1966
Martin Luther King Jr. leads an integrated march in Chicago and is wounded when whites throw bottles and bricks at demonstrators.

October 1966
The Black Panther Party (BPP) is founded in Oakland, California.

December 1966
SNCC votes to exclude whites from membership.

February 25, 1967
Martin Luther King Jr. delivers his first speech devoted entirely to the war in Vietnam, which he calls "one of history's most cruel and senseless wars"; his position causes estrangement with President Johnson and is criticized by the NAACP.

May 4, 1967
Alabama sheriffs James Clark and Al Lingo are among those who fail to get renominated in Democratic primaries that have significant black participation.

May 10–11, 1967
Rioting at all-black Jackson State College in Mississippi leads to one death and two serious injuries.

June 13, 1967
Thurgood Marshall is the first black to be nominated to serve on the Supreme Court.

June 19, 1967
A federal judge orders Washington, D.C., schools to end de facto school segregation.

July 1967
Rioting in the black ghetto of Newark, New Jersey, leaves 23 dead and 725 injured; rioting in Detroit leaves 43 dead and 324 injured; President Johnson appoints Governor Otto Kerner of Illinois to head a commission to investigate recent urban riots.

February 29, 1968
The Kerner Commission issues its report, warning that the nation is "moving toward two societies, one black, one white—separate and unequal."

March 18, 1968
Martin Luther King Jr. travels to Memphis, Tennessee, to help settle a garbage workers' strike.

April 4, 1968
Martin Luther King Jr. is assassinated by James Earl Ray in Memphis, Tennessee, precipitating riots in more than one hundred cities.

April 11, 1968
Congress passes civil rights legislation prohibiting racial discrimination in the sale or rental of housing.

May 11, 1968
Ralph Abernathy, Martin Luther King Jr.'s successor as head

of the SCLC, leads Poor People's Campaign in Washington, D.C.

October 30, 1969
The Supreme Court replaces its 1954 decision calling for "all deliberate speed" in school desegregation by unanimously ordering that all segregation in schools must end "at once."

1971
The Supreme Court grants federal courts the authority to order busing to desegregate public schools.

1984
Jesse Jackson launches a campaign for the U.S. presidency.

1992
Riots break out in South Central Los Angeles after an all-white jury acquits four white police officers who were video-taped beating African American motorist Rodney King.

1995
Legions of black Americans gather in Washington, D.C., to participate in the Million Man March.

For Further Research

Books

Ralph Abernathy, *And the Walls Came Tumbling Down*. New York: Harper & Row, 1989.

Jervis Anderson, *Bayard Rustin: Troubles I've Seen: A Biography*. San Francisco: HarperCollins, 1997.

Jack Bass and Walter De Vries, *Transformation of Southern Politics: Social Change and Political Consequence Since 1945*. New York: BasicBooks, 1976.

Albert P. Blaustein and Robert L. Zangrando, eds., *Civil Rights and the American Negro: A Documentary History*. New York: Trident Press, 1968.

Taylor Branch, *Parting the Waters: America in the King Years, 1954–1963*. New York: Simon & Schuster, 1988.

Clayborne Carson, *The Autobiography of Martin Luther King, Jr.* New York: Warner, 1998.

Clayborne Carson, ed., *The Movement: 1964–1970*. New York: Greenwood, 1993.

Daniel S. Davis, *Mr. Black Labor: The Story of A. Philip Randolph, Father of the Civil Rights Movement*. New York: E.P. Dutton, 1972.

W.E.B. Du Bois, *The Souls of Black Folk*. New York: Dodd, Mead, 1979.

Dwight Lowell Dumond, *Antislavery: The Crusade for Freedom in America*. Ann Arbor: University of Michigan Press, 1961.

John Egerton, *Speak Now Against the Day: The Generation Before the Civil Rights Movement in the South.* New York: Knopf, 1994.

James Farmer, *Lay Bare the Heart: An Autobiography of the Civil Rights Movement.* New York: Arbor House, 1985.

Phillip S. Foner, *Frederick Douglass.* New York: Citadel, 1964.

Leon Friedman, ed., *The Civil Rights Reader: Basic Documents of the Civil Rights Movement.* New York: Walker, 1968.

Paula Giddings, *When and Where I Enter: The Impact of Black Women on Race and Sex in America.* New York: William Morrow, 1984.

Peter Goldman, *The Death and Life of Malcolm X.* Chicago: University of Chicago Press, 1979.

Grace Elizabeth Hale, *Making Whiteness: The Culture of Segregation in the South, 1890–1940.* New York: Pantheon, 1998.

Vincent Harding, *There Is a River: The Black Struggle for Freedom in America.* New York: Harcourt Brace Jovanovich, 1981.

Thomas E. Harris, *Analysis of the Clash over the Issues Between Booker T. Washington and W.E.B. Du Bois.* New York: Garland, 1993.

Stanley Harrold, *The Abolitionists and the South, 1831–1861.* Lexington: University Press of Kentucky, 1995.

Len Holt, *The Summer That Didn't End.* New York: Morrow, 1965.

Elizabeth Jacoway and David R. Colburn, eds., *Southern Businessmen and Desegregation.* Baton Rouge: Louisiana State University Press, 1982.

Martin Luther King Jr., *Why We Can't Wait.* New York: Harper & Row, 1963.

Stephen F. Lawson, *Black Ballots: Voting Rights in the South.* New York: Columbia University Press, 1976.

John Lewis, *Walking with the Wind: A Memoir of the Movement.* New York: Simon & Schuster, 1998.

Leon F. Litwack, *Trouble in Mind: Black Southerners in the Age of Jim Crow.* New York: Knopf, 1998.

Thurgood Marshall, *Dream Makers, Dream Breakers: The World of Justice.* Boston: Little, Brown, 1993.

August Meier and Elliott Rudwick, *From Plantation to Ghetto.* New York: Hill & Wang, 1976.

Milton Meltzer, *The Black Americans: A History in Their Own Words.* New York: HarperCollins, 1984.

Aldon D. Morris, *The Origins of the Civil Rights Movement.* New York: The Free Press, 1984.

Stephen J. Oates, *Let the Trumpet Sound: The Life of Martin Luther King, Jr.* New York: Harper & Row, 1982.

Paula F. Pfeffer, *A. Philip Randolph: Pioneer of the Civil Rights Movement.* Baton Rouge: Louisiana State University Press, 1990.

Fred Powledge, *Free at Last: The Civil Rights Movement and the People Who Made It.* Boston: Little, Brown, 1991.

Bayard Rustin, *Down the Line.* Chicago: Quadrangle, 1971.

Arthur Schlesinger Jr., *A Thousand Days: John F. Kennedy in the White House.* Boston: Houghton Mifflin, 1965.

Bernard Schwartz, *Inside the Warren Court.* Garden City, New York: Doubleday, 1983.

Booker T. Washington, *Up from Slavery.* New York: Doubleday, 1901.

James M. Washington, ed., *A Testament of Hope: The Essential Writings of Martin Luther King, Jr.* San Francisco: Harper & Row, 1986.

Juan Williams, *Eyes on the Prize: America's Civil Rights Years, 1954–1965.* New York: Viking, 1987.

Harris Wofford, *Of Kennedys and Kings: Making Sense of the Sixties.* New York: Farrar, Straus & Giroux, 1980.

C. Vann Woodward, *The Strange Career of Jim Crow*, 3rd ed. New York: Oxford University Press, 1974.

Jean Fagan Yellin and John C. Van Horne, eds., *The Abolitionist Sisterhood: Women's Political Culture in Antebellum America.* Ithaca, NY: Cornell University Press, 1994.

Andrew Young, *An Easy Burden: The Civil Rights Movement and the Transformation of America.* San Francisco: Harper-Collins, 1996.

Whitney M. Young Jr. *Beyond Racism: Building an Open Society.* New York: McGraw-Hill, 1969.

Web Sites

Africanaonline, www.africanaonline.com. This Web site offers extensive information on African American issues, including the civil rights movement and its leaders. Biographical information, primary source material, and articles are available.

The History Net/African American History, http://Afroamhistory.com. This comprehensive site maintains information and links to other sites about the events, leaders, and court cases that impacted the civil rights movement.

The King Center, www.thekingcenter.org. The center was established in 1968 by Coretta Scott King to promote the legacy of Martin Luther King Jr. and the civil rights movement. It offers a wide variety of programs and educational resources, including the King Library and Archives, the world's largest repository of primary source material on King and other leaders.

Malcolm X: A Research Site, www.brothermalcolm.net. This Web site offers information on the life and legacy of Malcolm X, including texts of some of his famous speeches.

Index